Spiritual

Interpretation of

Scripture

Joel S. Goldsmith

© Copyright 2008 – BN Publishing

www.bnpublishing.com

info@bnpublishing.com

Contents

Chapter 1
Introduction

The essence of this book is that God is. We talk about God; we think about God; we even pray to God. As we come into the conscious realization of God, we begin to see why talking about God is useless, and why much of our thinking about God is fruitless. God is the only reality of our being. He is our Life, our Mind and Spirit, the animating Principle, the substance and Soul of our being and yet — how well do we know God? In our experience we are apt to be content with the intellectual acceptance of God as Mind and Soul, and we fail to grasp that our great need is to know God — to understand the law and reality of our being. Men generally have little confidence or peace until they have a good position, or a successful business, or perhaps some land or investments. Then they achieve a sense of security and well-being, even though it is a known fact since human history began that these possessions are temporal and not permanent. The loss of them leaves men without hope in the world or in themselves, and the fear of losing them is the reason for most of the ills of the world, which are not brought about by the struggle to gain them. Those who find God, who attain even a small measure of understanding, have wealth that neither time nor circumstance can affect. These have no concern for their material or physical well-being, because they have found that their permanent and unchanging good, their invariable life and substance are all included in God. Let us not be satisfied with an abstract God, a God who we call by name and yet with whom we have no conscious relationship. If God is the only reality of our being, can we any longer delay real acquaintance with Him? To know Him aright is Life eternal. To understand Him is to know the security and peace "that passeth understanding." "Seek ye the Lord while he may be found." God is not found in names or statements of Truth. "He is in the midst of thee" — "He is closer than breathing" — yea, He is not in the physical sense of life, but is found in the stillness of your being when thought is tranquil. This does not mean that we are to forsake the world, but to abstain from the noise and clamor of everyday living, so that these do not cause even a ripple on the waters of thought. The spiritual sense of Scripture alone reveals the laws and lessons of the Bible by which we may live. This book is an introduction to that infinite theme. To live out from Soul Consciousness is to know and enjoy the beauties and joys of Life. The Science of Soul reveals the nature or spiritual healing and unfolds the activities and capacities of the Soul of the individual — of you.

The Nightingale of the East

Amidst the flowering plants of a garden in Egypt sat a nightingale of great beauty. Its soaring song filled the Oasis with lilting melody. Its song was a carol of love; a message of peace from out the heart of the Infinite stilling the waves of a world of sense. Knowest thou, Oh Bird, of the peace that fares forth with thy song? Knowest thou of the strife that is stilled by the melody from thy throat? Nay, the nightingale knows naught of the power of its song and less of the unrest that is quieted by its sound. So should ye be as the Song of God pours forth from you — the willing carrier of the divine message — yet unaware of the power of your being and still less aware of the troubled hearts ye quiet with your melody of love.

Chapter 2
Darkness to Light

Unless God shows forth our existence, we will labor in vain to make a success of life. So we take for a starting point the first verse of the 127th Psalm: "Except the Lord build the house, they labor in vain that build it: except the Lord keep the city, the watchman waketh but in vain."

It is possible to achieve great things in life through human means. Men have become wealthy, risen to great political and military power, achieved great things with the human mind and will, but in many cases the results of human effort have not been permanent or have not given the happiness that was promised.

Unless God produces for us, the product is apt not to be lasting or satisfying. When God produces for us our work is fruitful and brings happiness and joy with it.

What is happiness? George Bernard Shaw writes: "This is true joy in life: the being used for a purpose recognized by yourself as a mighty one. The being thoroughly worn out before you are thrown on the scrap-heap; the being a force of nature instead of a little clot of illnesses complaining that the world will not devote itself to making you happy." In his comment of Shaw's wisdom, John Mason Brown writes: "What happiness is, no person can say for another; but no one, I am sure, can be happy who lives only for himself. The joy of living comes only from immersion in something—anything—bigger, better, more enduring, worthier than we (humans) are. People, ideas, causes—these are for the one possible escape—not merely from selfishness, but from the hungers of solitude and the sorrows of aimlessness. Don't turn your back deliberately on the procession. Existence is a strange bargain. Life owes us little, we owe it everything. The only true happiness comes from dedicating ourselves to a purpose."

Indeed, you are here as a part of a great cause. You are that place where God shines through. There is no way for God to express Itself finitely. You are infinite. In realizing your true identity, you no longer have a selfish motive. You have nothing to get because you already have the power of that infinite One; therefore, the purpose of your unfoldment is that you may be a revelation to those who have not yet awakened to that truth. You are here as a part of that cause. Your purpose is to be the Light; to let that Light shine, that those who are not yet illumined may find in you a hope. Through the search for Truth you know God as Mind, Spirit and Principle or Soul, but in thinking of God in this light you are apt to think of Deity as universal Mind or Life separate or apart from yourself. This is the first correction to be made in your unfoldment of Scripture. You now recognize God to be the Mind or Soul of the individual, of you and of me. God is the Life of you and of me; God is the Principle of your being. There is no Soul, Spirit, Life or Mind outside of or separate from you. There is but one Life, the life that you are living now and that Life is infinite and eternal. There is only one Soul, your Soul—"closer than breathing, nearer than hands and feet."

It is only when we understand God to be our own Spirit that we can rest in the assurance that the Mind of me is always performing its infinite and individual activity. When you understand this, you do not have to direct this Mind, or petition this God which is Mind, to do your bidding. You do not have to outline what its course or procedure should be. You know that the very Mind of you is God, infinite intelligence, and you can trust it to fulfill itself. "*If* God knows our need"—this thought can only come to you if you are thinking of God as something apart from yourself. The reason for emphasizing this is that until you understand that you yourself are this infinite spiritual consciousness, you will not grasp the premise of the great truth: I am the Book of Life.

It must be true that since you are infinite consciousness, you embody within yourself all that exists—you include the entire universe within your being. The Bible, the Book of experiences of men, women, and ages of history, all is contained within the infinite, individual spiritual consciousness that I am. The Bible is not a book outside of you; it is not a series of events which took place thousands of years ago. Scripture is the unfolding of characters and movements or happenings that are taking place within you—right this minute. Every Biblical experience can be found in your consciousness at some time or other. You, therefore, embody within yourself every Bible of the world, every philosophy, character and story.

There are no mortals, no human beings; you are immortal. All that exists lives within your consciousness. You will never be characters or people in ancient Scripture; you will always live your present experience. True, it will be progressive. You are always unfolding in that place where you recognize that I am "I". You are there now, but you are unfolding individually toward the recognition of that point. I am the Bible, the Book of Life. The entire history of life is revealing itself as your consciousness. It may appear as a past, the present, or future, but it is really the Here and Now unfolding to your awareness. It portrays the qualities of your own thoughts, the activities of your consciousness. If you are ever betrayed, it is because in your consciousness there is still some quality of thought betraying you. Every bit of error that happens to us in our experience is directly brought on by some state of consciousness of our own. Not that "right thinking" stops it nor "wrong thinking" causes it, but in individual consciousness are these latent traits and they set these events in motion.

The stories of Adam and Moses, are only of value to you when you discover their relationship to your life; the laws of Scripture only benefit you as you realize them to be laws unto your affairs.

From the moment that Moses realized, "I AM THAT I AM" he was master of every situation, a leader of men. He knew then that life is not a physical experience, but is expressed as states and stages of consciousness and that progress is always from the lowest to the highest, to the realization that I am eternal Life.

The Book of Exodus, in which Moses leads the Jews from the lowest state of consciousness, represents the transition from bondage, ignorance and slavery into a higher form of humanity and a greater degree of human good.

In the forty years of desert experience, we go forward and fall backward; we go up and fall down; we progress and have backslidings—but with every experience we develop more faith, hope and courage.

The journey is in reality one from sense to Soul and all the events of the desert tour and detour, will eventually bring us into spiritual revelation.

There are three states of consciousness which you will meet in the Bible. First is the Egyptian darkness. Egypt signifies the darkness of ignorance, obscurity. (Metaphysical Bible Dictionary of *Unity.*)

This is where you find the Hebrews when they are slaves under Pharaoh. They are in a state of total ignorance of spiritual truth. They are without cultural or educational enlightenment; economically poverty stricken; in every manner hopeless and without even material good. In this Egyptian darkness there is bondage to physical sense, to bodily pains and bodily pleasures. There is the belief of power in material forms of supply and a slavery to matter as supply.

This may all be likened to your own state of consciousness before you received the first glimpse of Truth. You, too, are then in Egyptian darkness, spiritual ignorance and poverty, the darkness of your own consciousness before the advent of Moses in your thought. Moses is that state of thought in you which leads you out of the depths of utter lack to a higher and freer sense of good.

Into the darkened sense comes this first ray of Light with its Promise of a Land of Milk and Honey—a promise of abundance and joy.

Whatever it is that first brings us this Promise, it is our Moses—the Moses of the Bible or Book of Life which I am. As you follow that new Leader, the higher thought that has entered your consciousness, you are led into greater supply, better health, freer living. Every human circumstance is improved. The entire advance, however, is along the line of human betterment.

This period in your experience is the first introduction to Truth or metaphysics. The promise given you is better health or more wealth—and this, in most instances, is fulfilled.

However, it makes no difference how much material health or wealth you achieve—there is an end to it. There is no permanence to physical health or wealth. As in the Hebrew's desert experience of going forward and backward, out of slavery into freedom and often back into slavery, so in your desert experience, there is health and sickness, abundance and lack. The only permanence of health, harmony, peace and prosperity is in spiritual enlightenment. The spiritually enlightened are never poor, never dead—because the temporal and finite sense of life has given way to the permanent and real.

The second state of consciousness is human good—human betterment—human freedoms. This in turn is outgrown as the third state of consciousness is achieved, that which is called The Promised Land or the Kingdom of God. You come into this spiritual realm as you lose faith and dependency on things in the external, and as you lose hate and fear of persons and conditions.

During the Exodus, the journey from darkness to Light, you have the law as your guide, protection and supply.

Chapter 3
The Law

The First Commandment, "Thou shalt have no other gods before me," is an admonition to look to one source for our good and it indicates that Me or I AM is that source. To this law all must render obedience. I am the one who must obey it. If I lived in the constant awareness of my true identity, it would be impossible for any one to interfere with my demonstration of harmonious, fruitful and eternal life, and if men always heeded the First Commandment, the journey into the Kingdom of God would be a quick one.

Obedience to this command requires strict mental discipline. It means that every time you are tempted to place confidence in a power outside yourself, you must mentally argue with yourself (use the law) until you have brought yourself back into the presence and power of your own consciousness. This mental warfare is the law — the letter of truth — and always leads to the Spirit of Truth when faithfully followed. This, the First Commandment, then, is a law which you must literally obey — have no other presence or power than the Universal Consciousness, this is the consciousness of the individual, of you. You exist as infinite, individual, spiritual consciousness. You are not body. You are not limited mind or mentality. You are consciousness.

What is this "I" which possesses body, business, home, talent, genius? It is not body. Feet, arms, legs, head —these are mine. But what is this "I" or "Me" that possesses them? There is only one "I", one Ego, one Consciousness. It is God. "I" am therefore universal. It is the "I" of me —individual Ego appearing as you, as me, as all so-called individual men and women. Individual existence is the continuous unfoldment of experience from within your own being. Nothing and no one exists outside your own consciousness. What we behold as person and thing is the idea of reality unfolding as our consciousness.

There is in all the universe but one power, and I am that law and power. The consciousness which I am, the only I or Me, this is the only power and therefore all power is good — and beside Me there is no power. Every evil is, therefore, a misconception of the one power, the all good power that I am.

There is no condemnation when you are under a belief of error, whether it is of sin or of sickness. There is no error personal to you. All error is a universal belief which we accept and therefore manifest. It is this acceptance of universal beliefs which causes you to believe you are sick or sinful.

There is only one power. This is the significance of the First Commandment. To fear or hate another power is to forfeit your God bestowed dominion.

There is no such thing as good overcoming evil; nor God healing your diseases; nor God reforming sinners. Overcome false theology here and now by accepting the First Commandment.

The Bibles of the world tell of two powers, of good and of evil — but that is because Scripture has been accepted from the standpoint of literal translation instead of read in the light of spiritual inspiration.

Scripture should not be interpreted merely as historical documents, but as the spiritually revealed Truth of inspired sages and seers. In this Light there is but one presence, one Power — and I am that.

In this spiritual Light, you find Universal consciousness, the Kingdom of Heaven; you find Grace and spiritual freedom. Here there are no battles, no mental powers, no opposites and no opposition. "Not by (physical) might nor by (mental) power, but by my Spirit." Immortality without effort.

Have no other consciousness but the universal, which is the infinite consciousness of the individual. Realize the omnipresence and omnipotence of the invisible Reality. Understanding God as all does not deprive you of individuality. You do not lose individuality or personality by impersonalizing your sense of good.

Do not attempt to annihilate God's infinite individuality which is expressing as your particular personality. God being infinite must express Itself as infinite individuality and this gives each one his own particular personality, or the consciousness of his individual being. A blade of grass never becomes a rose, a cat or a star. Always, throughout eternity each is maintained in its own individuality. Never subdue yourself. Let yourself come out. Never be afraid to be different. Always be yourself. Only in freedom can you be yourself. Assert your individuality.

You are not learning more Truth. You are revealing, unfolding as infinite individual consciousness and you are the Light of the world. There is only one Truth and — I AM THAT — and it appears as infinite facets.

The Ten Commandments are stepping-stones to Universal consciousness. To make the transition you must for a while dwell tirelessly on these injunctions, just as in mental treatment you may affirm the truths and deny the errors.

The First Commandment is: There are no other gods or powers — there is but one Presence, Power and Law, and the divine or infinite Consciousness, the consciousness of the individual, is that Power.

Second Commandment: "Thou shalt not make unto thee any graven image." This law calls for you to refute mentally any suggestion of power in matter, mortal concepts, medical beliefs, theological theories, rites, ceremonies. It means that you must recognize what you see, hear, taste, touch or smell as finite concepts of Reality; therefore, you must not love, hate or fear that which is visible to sense, but realize the omnipresence of the invisible Real even while this Reality is not apparent to sense. It means that you are not to worship any human concept appearing as person or thing — regardless of how good or noble. "Why callest thou me good? none is good, save one, that is, God." (The Invisible, of which the visible you is the finite concept.) *Anything external to sense is the concept and is not be worshipped, hated, or feared.*

Definite fears exist in the thought of many: fear of sin or its consequences: fear of disease and its ultimate effect: fear of the thoughts of other people. Remember that this is idolatry. There is only one Power, and that is the Mind which is the Mind of the individual — of you — and that Mind is the only law unto you and unto all that concerns you.

With this realization there can be no such thing as malpractice, or the transfer of evil thoughts of an individual exercising mental influence upon another. If one accepts the belief that another's thought can control him, he has not attained the realization that there is but one Power and that the Mind of himself is that Power. Malpractice is the only basis of error, but this universal mesmerism disappears in the light of the First and Second Commandment.

Third Commandment: "Thou shalt not take the name of the Lord thy God in vain." Do not identify spiritual Reality as a mortal concept. You and all that comes to your consciousness as person, place or thing, is divinely Real —yet as it appears through the testimony of the five senses, it is illusion or mortal concept.

Fourth Commandment: "Remember the Sabbath day to keep it holy." This Sabbath has still another meaning for us: "in it (Sabbath) thou shalt not do any work." In this Sabbath state of consciousness we do no mental work — we "take no thought" — we give no mental treatments for healing sin or disease. We rest and *let* God work in us, through us or, more rightly speaking, *as* us. It is a mental relaxing and a "thank you God, I am" — "Speak, thy servant heareth." — a letting go.

Fifth Commandment: "Honor thy father and thy mother." There is but one creative Principle and it is Father-Mother to Jew and Gentile, white or black, yellow or brown, man, beast, animal or plant — and that Principle or Consciousness I AM.

To *rightly* honor this causative principle, we must see it in all things: we do not recognize men as enemies; nor do we believe in ferocious beasts, harmful reptiles or poisonous plants. It requires mental discipline (during the period of our Exodus) to keep thought in line with this truth.

Sixth Commandment: "Thou shalt not kill." This Commandment does not deal with evil person or thing. There is nothing outside of your consciousness — and you would find no occasion to destroy anything within your own being. As Consciousness, your consciousness, embodies the universe, there is to you no evil person or thing. Only Truth fills Consciousness, therefore, do not attempt to injure, kill or exclude Truth or its ideas by entertaining a false concept of anyone or anything. Do no accept the suggestion of a selfhood apart from God — or you will, in belief, be shutting out the true idea. As your consciousness is filled only with Truth and its ideas and activities, do not, in your thought, destroy any sense of reality by admitting false conclusions, erroneous concepts or evil suggestions. On the other hand, Truth itself (your consciousness) is a law of destruction to every belief or concept unlike itself.

Seventh Commandment: "Thou shalt not commit adultery." Adultery is being false to a trust. To be false, to betray a trust or truth, is to betray God — which really means to leave God, Truth, and Life, for idols, lies and death. To behold less than perfection is adultery. To attribute qualities of good to material or mental concepts is also adultery. Let us have the single eye.

As there is no one and no thing outside your own consciousness, loyalty to a trust or truth has nothing to do with human relationships. It has to do solely with beholding perfection as perfection; with seeing wholeness, completeness and harmony as the truth of being. Eighth Commandment: "Thou shat not steal." As you are all-inclusive Spirit, substance, reality — as you are the infinite consciousness, embodying within yourself the universe, there is nothing to steal and no one from whom you can steal. There is not anything to desire or to demonstrate.

You are the fulfillment — the presence of God's all ness. Then theft, or even the desire for something outside oneself, is a belief of separation, which is belief in God *and* man, instead of the understanding of God manifested as the individual, or Life expressing itself as man.

The belief of being robbed is also a belief of selfhood apart from God. The temptation is to believe there is a thief — a selfhood apart from God, and one who is robbed — another selfhood apart from God, whereas what appears as the thief or the one robbed — all this is God — the One appearing as many.

This Commandment is an injunction to remember your true identity as individual infinite consciousness, including within yourself all good.

Ninth Commandment: "Thou shalt not bear false witness." This is a continuation and elaboration of the Eighth Commandment. The only way to bear false witness is to behold a selfhood apart from God.

Tenth Commandment: "Thou shalt not covet." This is also a continuation and elaboration of the Eighth Commandment, "Thou shalt not steal."

These Commandments constitute the law of Moses, or letter of truth, and they are steppingstones to the spirit of truth, which is the kingdom of God, the Promised Land or Universal consciousness. To make the transition from the law to the Spirit, we must for a while dwell daily in thought on these injunctions.

Chapter 4
Spiritual Sense of Truth

"Except the Lord build the house, they labor in vain that
build it." — Psalm. 127:1

Regardless of the human effort we put into any enterprise, if it is not backed by spiritual awareness, all we can expect from it is limited fruitage.

There is a vast difference between statements of truth and Truth itself. A statement of truth is what you declare: Truth itself is what is imparted to you from within your being. Statements of truth are read in books; Truth itself is what you discern between the lines.

Shankara, probably 800 B.C., wrote: "If the supreme truth remains unknown, the study of scripture is fruitless; the study of the letter alone is useless; the Spirit must be sought out by intuition."

The human mind claims to be a builder, to be a power, claims that it can do things for us. For generations the world has gone on trying to build humanly, and all it has accomplished is limitation. To insure the safety, security and prosperity of our existence, we have to come into the consciousness — the conscious awareness — of the presence of God.

Without this awareness, it is just as erroneous to make statements like, "God will help me; Got is ever-present and does help me," as it is to forget to make those statements. The statements themselves have no power. The human mind making such statements does not even believe in them. There must be an actual awareness of the presence of God. This must be felt within your own being.

Realize that you are but the instrument through which or really the being *as* which God acts. In every detail of your life turn to the one Mind, God, in order that you may be rightly governed. In the recognition that all decision is with God, you have taken a step in making practical a revealed truth of Scripture.

Many believe they are turning to God when actually they turn to a God they ignorantly worship. To avoid this error, you need to know God as the Mind of you, the consciousness of the individual.

You have received the revelation of God as the Reality of your being; therefore, in turning to God you are not running to some far off Deity, but to the infinite intelligence of your own being. You are putting your human, limited self aside so that this infinite Mind, which is God, your own Mind, may make its works manifest.

There are times when we make statements that are subject to misunderstanding. First, none of the statements, none of the affirmations, none of the denials we can make are helpful; because they are actions of the human mind and there is no power in them. "Take no thought for your life, what ye shall eat" — "Pray without ceasing" — " Know the truth and the truth shall make you free." These all seem contradictory. Yet, "take no thought" does not mean do nothing, for we bring into consciousness our oneness with God by taking thought. But it does mean not to take thought in the sense of making something happen, or using our thought as a power to bring something about that we desire. Our taking thought is a realization of a truth that is already true. Our praying without ceasing, or knowing the truth, is not declaration made to bring something about, to heal something, to enrich some one or improve some one. These are rather reminders of that which is already true. That is why, when we get past the stage of just making affirmations to make something happen, we are much busier and we work harder than ever before. When we had a problem and turned to statements, we kept up those statements until the problem was met, then we had a period of rest. But in this higher consciousness, there are no periods of rest, it is a twenty-four hour job of knowing the truth — not declaring the truth to make something true, but a constant realization of that which already is.

We do not take thought about demonstrating an automobile or a house or a healthy heart or eyes or ears: that would be taking thought for the physical, or realm of effect. We must take no anxious thought for what we eat, drink or wear, but at all times we must pray without ceasing. We must know our true identity: this is to pray. Begin by knowing that "I and God are one; that the inner Power is with us at all times to make the crooked places straight and the rough places smooth. Be conscious of your oneness with God —conscious that God is the Mind of the individual, whether that individual is you or some one else you have in thought.

We do this throughout the day, or when some immediate problem is on the scene. We do not let our thought dwell on fears or doubts, nor on the fact that the progress today may not be as rapid as we expected. Keep thought: stayed on Thee"; pray without ceasing. We must maintain within our consciousness the realization that all that the God has is mine.

The divine Mind, the creative Principle of the universe, is the one Mind, which is my Mind, the Mind of my neighbor, the Mind of my friend, and far and above all, it is the Mind of my enemy too. Only that universality of Mind will enable me to say, "the Lord is building my house; the Truth is making my demonstration."

The statement that "I and God are one" does not mean that a human being is God. But God is the Mind, the Life and Soul of me and I am not a human being. That which the world calls a human being is a false concept that it is beholding of me. What I see of you, which appears to be human, represents my concept of God, the one Life, the one Soul. If I am not beholding that, I am beholding God erroneously, the one Life erroneously, the one Soul and Spirit finitely.

The purpose of writing is not for one person to teach another. There is only one Mind and it is a sharing of the unfoldment that is coming through as that one Mind. There is not one person sitting up on a higher level of understanding than another. There is in reality no such relationship in the entire world as teacher and student. Mortal mind would love to set up teachers or "saviors" and take potshots at them. Mind is revealing its truth, the reality of its being to all of us simultaneously. This writing is merely a concession to our seeming ignorance of the fact that Mind is as effective in the silence as in the written word. God is the all of you — anything else is illusion. That means, that since God is all there is of you, there is not a discordant note within range of your voice. Let yourself look, not at a human being, but through to the Soul of him and say, "There is God." In this vision, there is no one too short, too tall, too stout, or too anything. Niagara Falls is still Lake Erie, when it is falling over the cliff: the name is merely a designation for that particular spot in that body of water. There is no such thing as "man" that is just a name given to God where God becomes visible and visibly understood.

There is no place where God ends and man begins. In that sense, God is the Life of you, the Soul of you, the Spirit of you. In the reality of me, I am God, but what you see sitting in a chair is but the transparency through which God is appearing. The eyes are called the window of the Soul —Soul is God. In this way, we are not apt to exalt human hood. Whatever of life, love, intelligence there is flowing through any individual is God and is necessarily greater than the individual, but yet One, just as sun and sunshine are one.

Chapter 5
Ruth and Naomi

Naomi is the individual soul when it is has failed to realize its oneness with God; it is seeking good in the material realm. Naomi may be the state of *your* being when, not rising to the spiritual consciousness in which you live, move and have your being, you start out to seek your good through material means and human beings. Your Soul is God, but when this sense of separation from good arises in you, and you start looking for good in the outer realm, in things or persons, that is when *you* are the Naomi state of consciousness, and when thus seeking, you are seeking it in Moab. The metaphysical interpretation of Moab is sense consciousness, or material sense.

Ruth, of course, represents the beautiful, the thought which loves the one good — spirituality. You have forgotten that "all that God hath is thine"; that you need not seek or labor for your good; that you do not even have to earn or deserve it. You need only realize that "I and God are one" —— heir with to all the heavenly riches. Then you would not have to suffer the experiences through which you now follow Naomi.

Naomi having left her divine state of spiritual consciousness in which is her eternal substance (Bethlehem-Judah) and gone down into materiality (Moab), now loses all her earthly possessions: husband, sons and lands. She has left, however, one spiritual idea, Ruth, and with this one Light within her consciousness, Naomi returns to her original home, spiritual consciousness (Bethlehem-Judah) and through Ruth realizes again her rightful consciousness, home and security.

Ruth, the spiritual Light, shines in all individual consciousness to show us and lead us to home, heaven or harmony. This Light appears now as Ruth, again as Moses leading the Hebrews to the Promised Land, the Kingdom of God within you, lifting you from sense to Soul.

Within each one, regardless of where he may be at any moment, there is always this spiritual idea, Ruth, who will cling to God regardless of how far down the ladder he gets mentally, physically, morally or financially. God is the Light within your own being; it is to you what it was to Elijah — the still small voice. Whatever name you give it, it is an infinite omnipresent Power; it will never leave you nor forsake you.

"Entreat me not to leave thee, or to return from following after thee: for whither thou goest, I will go; and where thou lodgest, I will lodge: thy people shall be my people, and thy God my God; Where thou diest, will I die, and there will I be buried: the Lord do so to me, and more also, if ought but death part thee and me." (Ruth 1:16, 17)

How do you awaken to the realization of the presence of God within?

You have come to this world in the belief that you are a human. You have grown up in this belief. You have been taught to turn to human sources and persons for aid. Your whole thought has been trained to look out into Moab, into the external world, for help, success, activity. You have not been told to depend on spiritual presence and power. Now, through metaphysical study and spiritual development, you have been turned within, given some idea of what really awaits you when you discover the Godliness of your own being. From this point on you must make this Power a living reality, a conscious Presence. It is a conscious process and is achieved through "praying without ceasing."

The first step for you is the continuous realization of your oneness with God — the realization of your true identity. Then comes the understanding of the nature of error as illusion, mirage, suggestion or nothingness. Prayer itself is the Word of God; therefore to be receptive to this Word means to learn to be still—to listen for "the still small voice."

While it is necessary to go through the mental process of realizing your oneness with God, take a few minutes in the morning and before retiring at night, sit down, without any declaration — just for a moment — and listen for that voice of Truth. This will lead you to the real sense of prayer —the Word of Truth making itself known to you.

When called on for help by another, try to forsake affirmations and denials. It is a sacred truth that God is the only healer. There is illusion to be dispelled, but it is folly to believe this can be done with the human mind or thought.

This is the attitude to be taken when asked for help: sit back, close the eyes and let the Word be made manifest to you. The work is done. The healing will take place because it is not dependent on the human knowledge of Truth — on the human understanding. It is reliance on God, on Truth itself, dispelling the illusion of sense. That Word of God is prayer. There is nothing in the world that cannot be accomplished by the Word received in thought.

Error, or evil, being unreal, an illusory sense, can never be externalized — can never be person, place or thing. You cannot live successfully and harmoniously until you realize the unreal nature of error as universal belief or hypnotism. Until then you will be fearing or hating some form of error. Illusion, regardless of the form it appears in — whether as person or condition — is not to be feared or hated, overcome or destroyed, but merely to be seen for its nothingness.

Sin, disease, death — these are not errors but the forms in which the one error, mesmerism, appears. Error is always illusion, though appearing as person or condition. Or it may appear as lack or limitation.

When error is handled or treated as mesmerism — nothing claiming or appearing to be something, it disappears. To fight error is fatal. Always what is appearing as evil is an aggressive mental suggestion, and with the realization of that, you have error destroying itself. Whenever you are faced with any kind of illusion, remember that it has no power to be anything except what it is — mirage or nothingness. To illustrate this nothingness of evil, we may well ponder the oriental story as given in The Infinite Way of the man who mistook the rope for a snake:

"About 500 B.C. it was written: 'It easily happens that a man, when taking a bath, steps upon a wet rope and imagines that it is a snake. Horror will overcome him, and he will shake from fear, anticipating in his thought all the agonies caused by the serpent's venomous bite. What a relief does this man experience when he sees that the rope is no snake. The cause of his fright lies in his error, his ignorance, his illusion. If the true nature of the rope is recognized, his tranquility of mind will come back to him; he will feel relieved; he will be joyful and happy. This is the state of mind of one who has recognized that there is no personal self, that the cause of all his troubles, cares and vanities is a mirage, a shadow, a dream."

To material sense, sin and disease appear as real entities having substance, law, cause and effect. To material sense both sin and disease seem personal and tenacious. But to spiritual consciousness both sin and disease are unrealities in the sense that they exist only as the product of universal belief of a selfhood apart from God.

To the metaphysician, healing of sin and disease are brought about in the degree of the realization of the infinity— the absolute all ness of eternal Life and its formations,
and of the unreal nature of error in every form.

Chapter 6
Spiritual Development

In proportion to the cultivation, development and unfoldment of your spiritual awareness of life, will harmony appear in your health, business and home life. There is no external change without an internal development. You may wonder as you go through the years with no apparent change in your affairs, why this thing called God isn't doing something for you. You can go on for your entire career and still find no increase or improvement unless there is inner expansion, a broadening of spiritual vision.

There must be a change in consciousness before there can be a change in your outer experience. When you turn to a metaphysician for help and receive it without having expanded your consciousness; you have been improved through his spiritual unfoldment. Sooner or later, in order to hold your good, you will have to realize your God-being; you will have to cultivate a spiritual sense of existence. Your good must come to you as the result of the activity of your own consciousness.

Every spiritual idea realized in your consciousness will find manifestation and expression. Not that the manifestation is external to you, but it becomes an object or expression of subjective unfoldment. This is law, a spiritual law: there can be no external change without an inner change. When your consciousness develops greatly, you are able to grasp the vision of spiritual life and its spiritual formations. You then discern "the temple not made with hands" — the spiritual body, health and wholeness.

The God that controls your destiny is your consciousness. You might say that it is divine Consciousness or divine Mind, and it would be true, but putting it that way, you are apt to think of it as something outside of or external to yourself.

One of the greatest factors in the failure of men is the belief that God is something other than their own being, and therefore, they are looking to something outside themselves to do or achieve for them.

Your whole existence is reconstructed by your consciousness of good. Always when you go into the temple of your being with a listening attitude, something takes place which we call realization and an outer harmony is revealed. You do not go within to tell God your desires or to outline the condition of thought to be changed — only to listen, to be receptive to the voice of Truth.

There are no evil powers to overcome, to be destroyed or removed. There is but one Power. I am that individual consciousness. I am the law unto my being. I am the government of my body and business. Because "I and God are one" and that one is God, I am the law of eternal harmony unto my universe.

Right where you are seeing me or I am seeing you, right there is the one Life, the one Soul, called God; infinitely appearing as an individual. Only in the realization of the one universal Life, expressing as you, can you experience immortality.

Only in this sense can you know abundance. No contact need be made with some principle or God, for you are this Principle, this Mind, and the realization of this truth starts the entire God-being flowing consciously *as* you. Truth appears *as* you. Life appears *as* you. Soul reveals itself *as* you. This truth is the truth of individual being — of you and me.

Starting with Genesis, the story of creation, you understand now there never was a God and a creation, nor a time in which creation began. Your consciousness unfolding is what is termed as God creating.

This does not make a God of our human or personal consciousness, nor give us a consciousness apart from the one universal Consciousness. Rather it reveals that Consciousness as the only creative Principle of the universe.

It likewise reveals the universe as the continuing unfoldment of ideas, without beginning and without end, and this revelation shows forth your immortality. Your so-called human consciousness is the shutter that keeps out the infinity of your own consciousness and, opening wider, let's in the realization of its infinity. When that shutter is completely open, there is no barrier —therefore, no separation or limitation. You cannot increase your consciousness because it is already infinite, but you can open your eyes in awareness of the infinite nature of your being.

You who come to the search for God are probably seeking healing of some kind—physical, mental, moral, or financial. Life must be understood as a giving process rather than a getting one. As we face life with this attitude, we draw spiritual riches from it in the form of health, harmony, supply, activity, home, companionship and purity.

Many fail to realize their desire because their thought is held to getting, achieving, accomplishing, rather than the unfoldment of good from within. When we bring to the search a heart full of love for God, for Truth, for Reality, all things are added unto us.

You need never seek your good outside yourself. It is true that your good comes to you apparently as a person or thing, or through some individual or circumstance. All good, however, comes through the realization of your Self completeness. This realization is your need.

Life is Self-sustained; individual life is Self-sustained. The belief in a power apart from God is duality. Since God is the Mind, Soul and Life of the individual, you are immortal and perfect.

The basis of a metaphysical healing is that neither sin, disease nor death exists as reality. They have no existence except as illusions of sense. It would therefore be folly to use any power — material, mental or spiritual — to over come or destroy that which has no real existence. Spiritual healing is the realization of oneness and that One God.

All that takes place in treatment is the practitioner's realization that all there is God.

There is only one infinity expressing itself. What then takes place in the thought of the individual when he goes into prayer, meditation or treatment?

You turn within to re-establish your realization of oneness. Temporarily you have come into the belief that I and God are two. The more you realize oneness, the more you consciously reflect infinity in your experience. You are separated from your good, or seem to be, through ignorance. If this were not so, all human experiences would be seen as divine. It is only as you give up the belief in a selfhood apart from God that you achieve the awareness of your spiritual identity and spiritual demonstration of life. Success crowns our efforts as we learn that God, practitioner and patient is one. But for this we would have God with infinite power of good, a patient lacking some form of good, and a practitioner with some mysterious power going to God on behalf of the patient for some good. There is no such relationship or condition in all history. Our sense of unity is the One appearing as many. Always God is God and includes all that appears as God, patient and practitioner.

You yourself are the law. The law is law only as you realize it within or as yourself. Making declarations of truth is not sufficient. It helps. Statements are reminders of your true identity, but the so-called demonstrations are never made until a feeling accompanies the letter of truth — until some inner conviction comes with it, some realization of a "peace be still" within your own being.

For too many years, Truth students and metaphysicians have been content with healings. The time has come to rise to a higher sense of Life. Yours must be the realization of the presence of God. Let this Truth provide the added things of health and prosperity, joy and freedom. Your good will always appear in the form necessary at the moment. It is not, however, a human good appearing but rather a spiritual idea upon which you are placing a finite interpretation.

As you realize your oneness with God, you will understand that there has never been a sick or sinning person. All disastrous things will continue to appear until you attain a realization of the true nature of your being, which is Spirit, God.

The experience of the Hebrews under Moses is one of fluctuating human good. This will be your experience as long as you live only in a realm of demonstrating things and conditions.

The Ten Commandments were laws of human good; governing human conduct. It is only as we come consciously into oneness with God that we attain the eternal harmony of spiritual good.

That which appears to sense is our concept of the eternal and real. The incorporeal and spiritual temple, body or universe is seen as finite, corporeal and material. This does not constitute two worlds, but one — the spiritual and harmonious. The sense world is not a world, but merely your limited sense of the infinite. What you see, hear, taste, touch and smell constitutes the illusory sense of Reality. Let us realize everything as God — appearing and any finite sense as the illusion.

When we see railroad tracks come together, the illusion is not "out there" at the tracks, but in our false and limited view of the perfectly placed tracks. The sky is not sitting on the mountain, and the illusion is not "out there" where it seems to be, but it is your false sense of what you are beholding.

You cannot get rid of the illusion; you must understand it as illusion, and see through it to ever present Reality. Understand that all that appears is God-appearing, despite the illusory sense of it you may be momentarily entertaining, and even the illusion will be dispelled. Error is never personal. You must therefore never condemn a person, but see the error as impersonal, a part of universal mesmerism and no part of any individual. In this impersonalizing of error, you dispel it.

Your understanding of a prayer of forgiveness is that it is the realization of oneness. To know that that which is appearing, as persecutor, hater, enemy in any form, is really God itself, which finite sense has misinterpreted, will free you of any evil effects of hate, persecution and enmity. Never forget that there is in reality no sick person to heal, neither a sinner to reform — only God to be spiritually discerned. This is the true law of forgiveness. Thus we pray for our enemies.

There is a prevalent belief that the thought of certain individuals or groups can harm you. You cannot be made to suffer from any belief other than your own acceptance of a selfhood apart from God.

Those who entertain a belief in two minds or in a life that can be impaired or ended, or in a selfhood apart from God, suffer from the belief in proportion as the belief is accepted. This, too, can be healed in a moment by a relinquishing the belief in two powers, and the belief in more than one Presence.

The purpose of your study is, first, the improvement of human hood — the improvement of health, wealth, harmony, companionship, home and security. The average person stops there, content. In their place of worship, marriage, business and body, they find an increased sense of good and then rest content, and because of this the problems of the world are never solved. At best they prolong their human sense of existence — put off the date on their tombstone by a few years.

The object of our search for truth is to gain a spiritual awareness of existence that we may live spiritually perfect and realize immortality without the change called death. In all the years of human history, there has never been peace even among neighboring nations; there has been no settlement of economic questions; there is still a battle between capitalism, socialism and communism.

No human government ever conceived is any better than the humans controlling it. The vision that is to come will only be when we transcend human hood and begin to live the divinity of our being.

All through the Bible you will find promises of the coming of spiritual man. The Bible contains many prophecies of the coming of spiritual man, Messiah. The belief is that these prophecies referred to the coming of one particular spiritual man. What value would it be to the world if all the Individual possible messiahs became Messiah — and we not? Many men have prophesied and predicted for centuries, but the advent of the Messiah is not the coming of a man who shall be perfect — but the coming of perfection in you and me.

Spiritually understood, the Bible is never personal, not even when it uses the names of people, centuries, cities and rivers, but rather these signify and symbolize spiritual qualities and activities of consciousness.

The only value of the prophecy of the coming of the Messiah is when it is understood to be the advent of the Messiah or Spiritual Consciousness to you and to me. The Messiah, this spiritual ideal, this spiritual consciousness, becomes evident as your individual consciousness, displacing the false or limited sense of self. It is a present reality awaiting in this instant your recognition and demonstration.

The Hebrews were always prophesying the coming of this Messiah. Not only those who follow the teaching of the Hebrew Law, but many Christians are actually Hebrews as long as they are prophesying or hoping for the coming of the Messiah.

According to Hebrew lore, the Messiah is still to come; according to Christian churches, the Messiah was among us for a brief period and ever since, the second coming is awaited. How hopeless the world must seem to both of these.

You can see that there never was a time that the Messiah was not present awaiting your recognition, and there will be no time when that Messiah will not be present as individual consciousness. We must acknowledge that the Messiah appears as individual you and me. Then we begin the demonstration of our spiritual existence and present immortality.

In the human thought there are stages of consciousness when the personal I, or ego, is paramount and we are engaging principally in the *getting* end of experience — getting, achieving, accomplishing, acquiring. Our existence then is directed towards what is coming in to us. Then there is the higher state of human hood where life is flowing out from us and we are more concerned for helping, sharing, teaching, co-operating.

The spiritual goes higher though than human good. In the spiritual life we are the Light of the world, and we are not concerned who comes into our orbit — how many, or if there are none at all. We are now the Light of the world, showing forth the harmony of spiritual existence, and allowing that perfection in us to attract those seeking something more than they have yet realized.

Chapter 7
Joseph

In Genesis we now come to the glorious story of Joseph, this includes the experience with his brethren.

For our purpose, spiritual interpretation, we understand that Joseph is that state of consciousness which is a developing or unfolding consciousness. As it unfolds, it reveals increasing vitality, substance and understanding. The Metaphysical Bible Dictionary of Unity says of Joseph: "The Lord shall increase; he shall increase progressively." That really is the progressive unfoldment of consciousness. As the story of Joseph unfolds, it reveals progressive steppingstones from potential good to a really advanced state of good human hood, and then finally the awareness of spiritual life and substance.

Joseph is our own ideal state of spiritual consciousness; it is that part of us which is pure Spirit — the embodiment of spiritual substance and wisdom. The many phases of being, found in individual consciousness, imply that there are other qualities in our consciousness besides this pure one, and those qualities are represented by the brothers of Joseph and by his coat of many colors.

This coat of many colors is supposed to be a very desirable thing, which has come to him as a reward or token of his goodness. I have seen this differently. To me this coat of many colors represents the many contradictory qualities in Joseph's thought. Joseph is a dreamer — yet the evil experiences which befell him outwardly, could only come as the result of inner conflicts and discords. Remember, Joseph is a progressive unfoldment of good, therefore, it must have progressed from something less than its later unfolded purity. These conflicting and contradictory thoughts are likewise externalized subjectively as his brethren.

Joseph, we read, goes down into Egypt; and you remember that Egypt is a place of darkness, sense consciousness, mortal mind, material experiences. Here is proof that along with the qualities of the dreamer, there are those other qualities outwardly pictured as his brothers. Reuben, unstable as water; Simeon and Levi, anger and cruelty; Issacher, a strong ass; Naphtali, a hind let loose; Benjamin, a wolf dividing spoil: all of this description is furnished by their father, Jacob.

These qualities of thought in human consciousness appear to do away with the good in us — the good which we would and do not.

Since these are the mixed qualities of Joseph's thought, we can understand the coat of many colors. Colors themselves symbolize qualities of character: red is for bravery; blue is for truth; yellow represents cowardice, and so on through all the colors. All of these are present in Joseph. Upon refinement, later, we meet the real Joseph in Egypt.

Before he was thrown into the pit, where he was left by his brethren, Joseph was stripped of this coat of many colors; the brethren took this coat with them. Is it not clear here that in this departure of the brethren from Joseph with the coat that the real meaning is that many of these contradictory states or qualities of thought have now been shed by Joseph. This new Joseph, progressively unfolding, is still the dreamer, yet with the worst phases of mortal belief overcome. He is now a better human, and his developed sense of human good now controls him and leads him into new and higher human experiences. Joseph's brothers hated him. These brothers, we have seen, were the erroneous human traits in opposition to the good. The good in your consciousness is likewise misunderstood and mistreated by the errors of human thought and would sell you into slavery to sense if you permitted it.

This might bring about a sense of condemnation unless you remember that neither good nor evil is personal. The fact that you may indulge error is not something for which you should condemn yourself as if you were responsible. These evils are universal beliefs, and if you have permitted them to use you, it is an opportunity for correction rather than condemnation. When you are cheated, acknowledge some erroneous trait still to be dispelled. Every evil experience that befalls you is the evidence of some belief not yet consciously thrown out of thought. You, like Joseph, are for the most part pure, but sometimes tempted by that in your consciousness which is impure or incorrect. These negative traits, when indulged, will land you in a pit, or send you, wanderers, into Egyptian darkness and despair: through indulgence we become their servants. That, however, which is the real Joseph to us will ultimately enforce itself in our consciousness and will free us of the entangling and sensuous beliefs which imprison us and hold us in bondage to limitation. You can follow Joseph (the pure state of your own consciousness) and watch it as, down through the years, it has been attacked by its brethren — conflicting qualities of thought in you. Perhaps you can see why you have been cast into a pit — why some erroneous trait has held you in slavery to some habit, sin or disease.

Now you are ready for the Messiah, the healing state of consciousness which is to rescue you and lift you into complete spiritual freedom and abundance. "So now it was not you that sent me hither, but God:" (Gen. 45:8). This idea is revolutionary. Up to now you have believed that your evil thoughts, traits and deeds brought you into punishment, slavery and bondage to sense. Now you learn that God has gone before you every step of the way, in order to get you out and set you free and make you a redeemer of men.

Here in Egypt, the slavery and prison experience is made to serve God's purpose. *From the moment that you no longer see evil in the circumstances governing you, you are seeing and acknowledging God as the moving factor in your experience, and only good follows.*

If you have God and one atom of something else, you have something outside the infinity of God. There cannot be God and even one iota of evil in the world, and therefore evil itself must be re-interpreted in order to be a part of the Kingdom of God. It cannot be left out of the Kingdom because you would have infinite God and something besides. Joseph acknowledged no presence or power apart from God when he declared, "So now it was not you that sent me hither, but God:"

You are faced with this same condition, and the moment you acknowledge that error has done this to you, you are lost. But, if you have the vision of Joseph and say, "No, error has not done this to me; error is not doing this to me; error has neither presence nor power," you will proved the all ness and omnipresence of God, good, and its immediate expression.

These are messages from God Itself. There is no night here — no night or dark places in your consciousness — but to recognize a presence of condition apart from God is to lose your way, at least temporarily.

Joseph, not yet raised to spiritual understanding, expresses his good humanly, as executive, business man, officer; but again he must be "pushed upstairs." Joseph's experience has not yet purged him of sense desire and so there are still the beliefs of lust, revenge and persecution to be overcome. Then, however, in one of his darkest prison moments, spiritual vision is awakened in Joseph, and his is lifted above all material conditions and limitations and is therefore able to discern spiritual abundance right where lack and poverty is claiming presence and power. Spiritual vision sets Joseph free, enables him to share the abundance of his vision and so overcome all mortal thoughts that he sets free all those brethren who come to him for aid.

These evil qualities now come to the liberated Joseph consciousness through others, called brethren, (or patients, students, seekers) and the Joseph in the liberated practitioner or teacher frees these others and spiritually feeds them.

"Now therefore be not grieved, nor angry with yourselves, that yet sold me hither: for God did send me before you to preserve life. So now it was not you that sent me hither, but God: and he hath made me a father to Pharaoh, and lord of all his house, and a ruler throughout all the land of Egypt." (Gen. 45: 5, 8)

You will understand this passage to mean that your spiritual consciousness carries you through the purification process, even though to sense you go down in the pits and prisons of sin and disease. Your enlightened consciousness goes always before you, carrying you through these trying and purifying experiences until at last your are father to Pharaoh: that is, supreme over material, finite sense; master of the corporeal sense and ruler over body and purse; a law unto yourself; and lord over all his house: that is, in complete control of your consciousness and its spiritual formations; and a ruler throughout Egypt: you are the Light, shining and dispelling the darkness of Egypt, or sense consciousness.

Chapter 8
From Law to Grace

"Except the Lord build the house, they labor in vain that built it." That which you receive through spiritual sense comes as the grace of God, and only this is important. Always, you must remind yourself of this, because it is impossible to *learn* spiritual reality. The mind is not capable of digesting spiritual Truth. Regardless of the words you hear or the statements you read, they are less than nothing in your experience until there is a realization within of the Truth of which the words can only *speak*. Literal interpretation of Scripture has created a God in a place called heaven, often pictured as if above the clouds over us; This has brought about the belief of separation between God and you making sense of duality which is responsible for every sin, disease and discord on earth. "I AM THAT I AM", reveals Moses.

The consciousness of the oneness of God and you, which we now interpret as God appearing *as* you, restores the lost Truth of all Scripture, re-establishes health, harmony, completeness and thereby ends discord and limitation. Exalting any of the historical characters of the world Bibles prevents the recognition of God being what you are. Looking outside yourself for the source of grace, you lose the real presence within.

There must, however, be a right appreciation of those men and women who attained a great measure of prophet as to become revelators of the truth of our being. These have all made great sacrifices of personal existence to reveal and teach the great Truth that I AM.

There must be gratitude felt in the heart, not merely expressed as lip-service, for the modern Teachers and Practitioners who have renounced personal life for the ministry of Truth. There must be a recognition of the sources and avenues of good; that is a part of gratitude and is a Godly quality.

Krishna and Shankara of India, Moses of the Holy Lands, are the ancients who have revealed the secret of the oneness of God and man, who battled the organized ignorance of their periods of history and sacrificed self for the privilege of revelation.

In modern times, Mary Baker Eddy repeated this revelation in the First Edition of Science and Health, and accepted the merciless persecution of pulpit and press to repeat this one wisdom, I AM.

There are strange happenings in the religious world today. Many books are being published, some of which have become best sellers, repeating the ancient wisdom. The realization is dawning in thought that there must be something more real than the letter of religion. Alvin Kuhn writes that this age will witness the Renaissance of ancient culture, and we see his words being fulfilled by the tremendous interest in such books as Cheney's, "Men Who Have Walked With God", Aldous Huxley's "Perennial Philosophy", and the many new translations of the Chinese Laotze and the Gita of India. Of what benefit will it be for men to turn away from outworn temple forms to the reading and study of the ancient and modern unorganized revelations? The first benefit is that of mental freedom. When men are no longer tied to superstition, obedience to man made rules of religious conduct — when men "feel" that they can, without fear of criticism and ridicule, open their thought to being taught of God — they really begin to live. Bigotry, racial and religious prejudice disappear as the old landmarks of "my church", "my God", "my creed" are realized as myths, superstitions and false theology. When men open their thought to Truth, they soon learn that there is but one God; that all men are the showing forth or presence of the One; that therefore, all spiritually are equal. The first fruitage of man's investigation of Truth will be the end of racial, religious and color bigotry. Another fruitage of the revelation of the oneness of God and man is the falling away of fear: the elimination of fear of lack, fear for health, fear of disease. Sin, likewise, or the desire for it, drops away in the consciousness of oneness with God. Since, "I and God are one", it is impossible that this "I that I am" should know lack, sin, or disease. In the realization that I am, there comes a sense of rest, of relaxing, of completeness and perfection. This in no wise exalts human hood, but, in the realization of your spiritual identity, the erroneous traits of human hood disappear. Opening thought to the search for Truth in the religious and philosophical literature of the world is but one step toward liberation from the evils of the world. Final release from sin, disease, death, wars, economic changes, comes only when the next two steps are achieved.

The first step may be termed the intellectual understanding of the truth of being, the first dawning in thought that I AM—not will be, should be, would like to—but I already AM.

The second step is an understanding of the nature of error. Throughout these pages the nature and character of error is told and re-told.

As long as attempts are made to cure disease, prevent sins or reform sinners, to halt lust, anger or revenge — the axe is not laid at the root of evil, and evil therefore will not be destroyed. The belief of a selfhood apart from God has created a host of beliefs and fears about and for this supposed personal selfhood, and these beliefs have become mesmeric in their intensity and action.

When we recognize that evil, regardless of whether it appears as sin, disease, lack, wars or death, is but one evil, mesmeric suggestion of hypnotism, we have found our freedom from these discords. In other words, the specific errors we behold or experience are not realities which must be fought or destroyed; they are not powers requiring some deific prayer or Personage to act; they are mirage or nothingness and need only to be acknowledged as such to reveal their impotence. This recognition is attained as our God consciousness unfolds and our spiritual sense of man and the universe expands.

Let us take as an illustration the vaudeville hypnotist who, as part of his act, invites members of the audience to come up on the stage to be hypnotized. Then he suggests to them that there is a white poodle on the stage which he wishes the mesmerized person to chase off into the wings.

Sometimes the white poodle goes off stage with little effort, but at other times it proves to be very obstreperous and difficult to make obey. Let us suppose now that our hypnotized friend recognizes help in removing his white poodle. Remember, to the hypnotized man the white poodle exists as a real entity, an actual presence, and he wants it removed. To the metaphysician, however, who is not hypnotized and sees clearly, there is no poodle there to be removed: only a mesmeric suggestion to be recognized as such, and this recognition brings the awakening and the disappearance of the white poodle. Thus, that is brought about which is termed healing.

In the same sense every problem, whether of health, supply, sin or fear, is real to the deluded sufferer, but to the metaphysician these exist only as the non-existent "white poodle" and he heals all manner of error through this understanding of the unreal nature of what *appears* as evil conditions of mind, body or purse.

The third step is the attainment of spiritual consciousness and this naturally follows the study and practice of the first two steps.

In the early days of metaphysical practice, the practitioner's understanding brought about the healings. There were at that time no text books on metaphysics, no temples or reading rooms or centers. The practitioner's understanding brought about the healing — or else there was no healing. If we accept that sense of practice today, we will have better results in our work.

The moment we attempt to impart Truth for the purpose of helping the healing work, when we ask a patient to read or go to the temple or attend a lecture with the idea that it will help or hasten the healing, we have forsaken the basic premise of our teaching: there is no reality to sin or disease, there is no erroneous person or condition to be changed, healed or reformed.

It is far better when we are called upon for help that we, as practitioners, assume the responsibility of realizing the present freedom of the so-called patient. Then, if there is a degree of receptivity, there will follow, in those who have been the recipients of the benefits of our understanding, the desire to know this Truth, to understand and eventually to preach and practice it. We cannot relieve any individual of the responsibility of studying and realizing Truth for himself.

Before the advent of Truth or of metaphysical healing in your experience, you were in a darkened state of thought — without spiritual illumination — without higher understanding. In this dark sense you were in bondage to physical pain and pleasure; to lack of peace and security, often in slavery to fear, sin and disease.

In the Bible we find the Hebrews under Pharaoh in just this state of ignorance, poverty and bondage. Into this blackness came Moses with promises of a better Land. To you Moses came as a promise of metaphysical healing, which was to lift you above the errors of sense — the same evils that bound the ancient Hebrews. In your case, as in the history of old, the promise was fulfilled with a better sense of health, supply, and freedom.

Under Moses the Hebrews experienced a greater area of land, more fertile land, on which to live, a greater freedom of physical movement. Also they enjoyed a freer sense of religious worship and a more abundant supply. All of this represents a greater degree of human good. So far though there is no spiritual development — even their religious worship is human form and ceremony.

There was also a constant fluctuation between good and evil, plenty and lack, freedom and serfdom, human good and human ill in their experience — further proof that their demonstration was wholly on the human plane.

As you look back upon your own experience in metaphysics or Truth, you will find that you also were only experiencing, even in healings, a greater degree of human good. You had not made the transition to the spiritual understanding which destroys the fluctuating experiences of humanhood.

No doubt many inharmonious physical and financial conditions disappeared to give place to physical conditions of harmony and increase. This was your Moses promise being fulfilled with greater human good. During this period of human improvement, you, just as the Hebrews of old, were under the law. Ten Commandments, rules and restrains — all these are necessary under the progressive steps with Moses. Moses, in your case, is the first promise in your consciousness of a better Land. You are no longer righteous because there is a law decreeing it; you are not good because there is regulation requiring it; you are not healthy because of some mental juggling; nor wealthy because of some miracle statements. You are, through God, the ever-present Spirit of God, lifted to Universal Consciousness or grace.

As you advance from Moses and improved humanhood, into spiritual consciousness, you touch the spiritual sense of health, wealth and harmony. In the Old Testament, it is good and evil, with good being invoked to overcome evil. In the Universal consciousness there is only the divine presence of God, one power, Good; one presence, Love; one condition, perfection. You only achieve the realization of the nothingness of evil as you attain spiritual consciousness. Moses represents that type of leadership which leads the unlimited human thought out of sense slavery into human good. In his teaching, Moses did not enter the Promised Land or spiritual consciousness. He never went beyond revealing human betterment.

If we think of these Hebrews as a slave race, illiterate, uncultured, uninspired, we now find them led out into a place of freer, better conditions, and to an obedience to the law. Even if you lived up to all the Mosaic laws ever written, you would at best be better humans only. Grace and Truth, spiritual freedoms, come only with Messiah or Spiritual Consciousness.

Universal consciousness sets you free from the desire for that which does not belong to you: sets you free from erroneous traits of character — from limitations of every sort. It is wonderful to realize that the man who is set free in God, who is free of all human entanglements, was at best only a short time before a good human! It is merely a transition form one sense or state of consciousness to another. All the experiences under Moses can be those of you and of me.

You are this state of darkened consciousness to which Moses, or the promise of Truth, comes bringing improved health, happier home and greater wealth; and you are that same consciousness to which comes the Messiah or divine idea, and sets you free as sons of God made flesh.

As the starved Hebrew's first thought is for more food, clothing, shelter, so do you in your first steps in Truth seek more and better matter. To God this thought of getting or achieving never comes. God feeds five thousand yet has not a thing laid by. It meets all needs through grace. How do you measure your spiritual progress? By the degree that your concern is not for gain, addition or multiplication, but rather that your understanding is grounded in the realization of omnipresence. As your conviction or confidence grows in the unfolding of good rather than in accretion — then you are coming into living by grace.

In this consciousness you realize, that God is always with you. You can measure your acceptance of the spiritual teaching by the degree of concern that you are losing about personal welfare. You must come to that place in consciousness where you live by grace, where you attain a measure of God and can always find yourself in the same relative condition of harmonious life regardless of any human changes that take place politically or economically.

Three states of consciousness have now been revealed to you. First was spiritual barrenness before the advent of Truth in your experience; then the Moses state of your consciousness in which you enjoy better health, more supply, greater freedom — although all of it is subject to chance and change, subject to superior human force; subject to loss, discord, depletion. There are no human guarantees.

Since you are seeking permanent peace, security and substance, you must find it in spiritual consciousness. You must raise yourself to the third degree in which you find Grace, in which you take no thought for the body, food or raiment

Chapter 9
Scriptural Symbols

Spiritual significance of Scripture is often revealed in the metaphysical interpretation of names of people of places, mountains, seas, and rivers we find in the Bible. The historical sense of the Bible is often not correct and is rarely of much important. The spiritual sense of Scripture is the important one, and it shows forth the laws and principles of harmonious existence.

Spiritual ideas and moral lessons have been interpreted as men, events and movements, and these must now be reinterpreted in order to unravel the mystery of the Bible and make Scripture practical in destroying its superstitions and mysteries.

People have considered their place of worship almost as important as the God they worshipped. The Holy Temple in Jerusalem was considered of such importance that Jews from all over the Holy Land made pilgrimages there every year. The Temple, however, rightly understood, is a symbol of the spiritual universe or body and is attained not by means of a pilgrimage from one place to another, but by an expansion of consciousness, which then includes within itself the secret of immortality or life eternal achieved here and now.

The material sense of Temple localizes and finitizes it; the spiritual sense reveals the infinite and immortal Temple of your life, your body, your experience of good.

This true view of Temple likewise spiritualizes your understanding of worship. Thinking of church as material, as having edifices and rules, materializes and finalizes and localizes worship, whereas, the spiritual sense of a temple reveals the unlimited, unfettered prayer uttered within your own being.

Following this line of thought, we find a Holy City, which, being interpreted, becomes divine Consciousness or and this is now understood as the consciousness of you and of me.

We likewise find in all Scripture an upper and a lower land, indicating heaven and earth, or states and stages of consciousness and symbolizing Spirit and body. There is always a connecting river and a bordering sea. The river is the individual path from sense to Soul, from the lower land to the upper, the bordering sea is either the troubled waters of material existence or the quiet waters of the Soul. Always there are smaller bodies of water to be crossed on the journey — the Sea of Galilee. Dead Sea, Black Sea, the Jordan — all symbolic of the one crossing from danger to safety, from matter to Spirit.

Within our own consciousness we find these places, rivers, temples and mountains—not outside of us in a book as it may appear. It is within our own consciousness that the rivers are to be crossed, the transition made from the localized and finite conditions to the infinite and omnipotent good.

In reading Scripture, remember that the people and events are to be understood as states and stages of your development and unfoldment, as spiritual consciousness. The tendency to translate spiritual ides of good into symbolic names of places is to be found in the naming of cities of the United States: Salem, Providence, New Haven, Newark, New Canaan, Bethlehem, Corpus Christi, Sacramento, and many others. No doubt the early settlers were expecting to find peace in Salem, security in Providence, a haven in New Haven, a new existence in Bethlehem, and so on down the long list of symbolic names. People always believe that they are going to find their peace, joy, health or wealth in some person or place—and that is one reason for so many disappointments. There is no such thing as a heaven to be found in person, place or thing. If we do not find our good in our own consciousness, we will not find it externalized, and if we do find it within our own being, we will find it wherever we may geographically find ourselves. No circumstance or condition can be experienced unless it first be found within our own consciousness.

"Except the Lord build the house, they labor in vain that build it." Unless the Consciousness of God speaks through us, it would not be the voice of God heard.

In every instance your interest must not be centered in or on the messenger, but rather in the voice of God and its message. You are always attuned, receptive to the ideas unfolding within you. Do not be enticed even by words of wisdom because the Spirit of God speaks in a spiritual tongue and interprets itself to the listener spiritually.

"Ye are the light of the world." That is your only reason for existing. Anything less would not be worthy of God's revelation of His own being.

God must play some part in our experience in order for us to receive the inflow of God. When we turn to God, let us try to rest, to let down the barrier of self to the degree that we acknowledge the divine Presence, the God Presence. There is no individual with more God Presence than another, yet there is a greater degree of awareness of the Presence in one than in another. Why turn to somebody else instead of the Kingdom within ourselves? Only because we have not given the time, attention, thought, prayer and consecration to the bringing forth of that Presence that some others have. Therefore, in our unlimited state, we may turn to another and there find the divine Grace. Finding it in some one else ultimately leads to finding it in our own being—because that Grace is the very Self of you and of me.

One of the puzzling things that faces every student of the Bible is the God of the Old Testament, the God of vengeance, the God that rewards and punishes. To me, the God of the Hebrew Testament was a blank puzzle for many years, and I could get nowhere in trying to fathom that God; yet at no time could I feel that something false or fictitious was being presented.

The same puzzle presented itself to me in the study of the three-faced Hindu God. How could these people that had such great light, such great wisdom, be so terribly wrong as to present a three- headed God: God the Creator, the Preserver and the Destroyer.

Now we have the answer, we know that the Hebrews and the Hindus both were right, because through the revelation of the spiritual sense of the Bible, we know that the destruction referred to was not the destruction of person, place or thing, but the destruction of the belief about the universe. Truth is a destroyer, but the only thing it has ever destroyed is error, and error never existed as a reality. We understand that God is a Divine Consciousness, Infinite Consciousness and, therefore, contains within Itself its all ness of being. We understand that nothing exists outside of God, that is outside of infinite Consciousness. It must be true, then, that God must destroy even a possibility of false concept. Within this infinite Consciousness which I am, there exists that which will destroy every illusory sense or concept. That is why we understand now that sin and disease do not exist as realities. They exist only as beliefs or false concepts, and it makes it simple for us to be healed of these errors, whether they are of health, morals or supply, when we realize that in the Infinite Consciousness we call God, there is that destructive influence ever ready to remove whatever is unlike God—not to remove person, place or thing, but to remove every false concept of person, place or thing. The Infinite Consciousness we call God is constituted of every quality of good, which includes always a force and power that is destructive to everything unlike its own being. This is an important thing at this particular time, because right now we are reaping hatreds due to the war, conditions national and international, racial and religious. We, though, do not have to be reformers. We have the realization within our own being, the Consciousness called God, and it has within Itself all that is necessary to destroy any qualities unlike good.

We do not have to be personal saviors to any one, because this infinite spiritual Consciousness, which is individualized has within Itself all that would be the Messiah, as well as all that is necessary to destroy all that is unlike good. We are never called upon to be personal saviors or punishers of evil doers. We can easily rest in the realization that God is the Mind, Soul and Consciousness of individual being. In this Consciousness is all that is necessary for the manifestation of the harmony of God being, as well as the destruction of everything that is unlike its own nature. That is why all through the Bible in the recorded healings, it is not in any way indicated that it is necessary to use suggestion or hypnotism in healing. It is not necessary to transfer thought from one individual who my be the practitioner, to another individual called a patient. The truth of being realized in individual consciousness is the law unto those who ask for help. We do not have to project our thought outward to a person, or even make them understand some truth. The metaphysician has no interest in truth as an abstract theory, but only as it is proved a practical way of life. The Word must become flesh; it must be embodied as our own being, it must make for us a joyous existence, a successful one, a happy one. The rule for all of this is laid down in the Scriptures of the world. We have seen how universal is Truth — in Oriental Scriptures, the Old and New Testaments, Emerson, Whitman — wherever we turn we find the same Truth, but we have not found it made practical in our own experience until the advent of metaphysical teachings within the last century.

Our turning to the Scriptures to find a solution to the problems in our individual experience is an example which may enable others to do the same. There is no way whereby we can save the world. This is entirely an individual experience. One of the sad parts of this is that at times we cannot bring our own families into it, as they can accept it only as they are ready. We can, though, be the light of the world: we can show forth, through our demonstration, that which will encourage others to seek the same way. That is as far as we can go. We can only show it forth and thereby encourage them to take the next step.

One of the points that has retarded our own healing work has been the inability to recognize the fact that it is not necessary to reach a person with our mental thoughts; it is not necessary to get a treatment across to a patient. It is necessary only to reach the depths of our own being, to have a realization within our own consciousness, and that is the point from this moment on we are going to remember. Healing has nothing to do with the other fellow; it has to do with our state of consciousness only. In these years that lie just ahead of us, that is the work that will have to be done to set the pace for the entire healing world. How do we spiritualize our own thinking so as to be the Light of the world? We have been taught that Truth cannot be known by the human sense; Truth cannot be intellectually discerned. Truth is a spiritual quality, and it must be spiritually discerned. It must enter our awareness through spiritual sense, through spiritual consciousness. This spiritual sense is attained in two ways:

one, by the reading of spiritual or inspirational literature, which, of course, includes practicing the truth learned, second, by contact with those who's thought is in the same direction. Spiritual consciousness is contagious: it is impossible to be in the presence of those who are making even the slightest degree of effort towards this awareness, without imbibing some of it from them. The greatest step is found in the word "receptivity," "Speak, Lord; for thy servant heareth." "Be still and know." "I will listen for Thy voice." Always it is *be still*; always it is listen; always the indication is to become receptive, open consciousness to the inflow. It is as if, just outside of our hearing ear, is an infinite reservoir of spiritual good, and by opening the ear, listening, we open consciousness for an inflow of the Word of God.

We have advanced to a state where our interest is in God and the things of God, where we must pray without ceasing; our lives must be a dedication. We are no longer living for ourselves, and that is not an understatement. It would be impossible to follow the line of work we have been doing if our interest was just self-interest. We have gone beyond that. We have come to a place of self effacement where we are living not for our own good: our demonstration is only incidental to the work that we are carrying on. "Ye are the light of the world." There is not an individual on earth who is not here as part of a divine plan. Every one has his own particular mission; every one here is to serve some particular part of God's purpose. As humans, we do not fulfill that mission—no human ever fulfilled a spiritual mission—but in the forgetting of our humanhood, divinity is revealed, the divine plan is revealed.

The public ministry of healing is only one avenue. Right where you are is holy ground — "the place whereon thou standest is holy ground" — and that is the place from which to show forth the Godliness of your being. Any further steps that have to be taken, will be taken by the godly part of your being. You will not have to plan it humanly.

Constant realization of the letter of truth is necessary so that we do not get lost in the bypaths of blind faith or superstition. It is much too easy to roll off the path into a blind faith, a superstitious faith. We must keep balanced; we must have a reason for our faith. This is not contradictory to the idea that we must be spiritually illumined, but rather, having a reason for our faith makes it possible to receive greater illumination.

To fall into a careless attitude of leaving it to God, without realizing that this God we are leaving it to is the reality of our own being, would be fatal to our ultimate demonstration. There is no God outside of our own being: God is the Mind of the individual, the Life, Soul and Spirit. Therefore, God is that which constitutes the individual. This being true, when we take the attitude, I can rest. I can relax, knowing that God is on the field, it is because we know that we are referring to our human sense of self that we can relax, knowing that the divine of us is on the field, knowing that the "I" of us is the law unto our own being, knowing that I and God being one, all that God hath is mine. Then we can relax and can even say, "Leave it to God." It is only when we fail to remind ourselves frequently of the true nature of God—of our oneness with God—that we are apt to relapse into the fatal belief of some power outside of our own being. We dare not accept the Bible as our guide, inspiration or textbook without accepting that I am one with God.

The Bible has not been so clear on the nature of error as the metaphysical writings that have been given to us for our study. It took deep spiritual insight to find that the evils and errors, the sins of the Old Testament, were not realities but negative qualities of thought. The literal study of the Bible does not reveal that, and that is why the clergy never taught it. All of them accept evil, error, as real. Error has been proved to be no more real than our own concept of it, so taking the Bible together with the metaphysical writings of today, we take another step in the realization of the letter of truth, because through this letter of truth, we are led to the Spirit.

You cannot accept intellectually the nothingness of error. In our study, we must understand the statement that error or disease is not real. We must gain some degree of realization of the nothingness of error. Words will not do it. The study of the literal sense of the Bible will not reveal the absolute Truth that there is but one Power. No matter how many times the Bible speaks of God as all, there are just as many references showing that evil has terrific power, and many times sufficient power to overcome good. But spiritual insight has revealed that the so-called evil powers were not powers but only beliefs, false concepts, ignorance. That leaves us, then, with the great task of getting used to the idea that there is but one Power and that that which is called evil is not power. As we accept this and apply it, ultimately we gain, through our sense of receptivity, a realization of that truth; and all the errors in the world are seen to be illusions, and we wonder that we ever feared them, or hated them, and in some instances, loved them.

Chapter 10
Universality of Truth

"Except the Lord build the house, they labor in vain that build it."

A Bible text is that on which we build our state of consciousness. We do not take Bible quotations and expect by much repetition for them to do something for us. We understand that every statement in the Bible that can be construed as a law must be embodied in and become a part of our consciousness in order that we may externalize the thought or idea in the text.

"Except the Lord build the house, they labor in vain that build it." We understand that the "Lord" in this case is our Consciousness. Our Consciousness is the law, is the constructor of our universe. Our Consciousness is the substance, the force, the fabric of which our entire experience is built, therefore, whatever we take into our consciousness and make a part of our consciousness, becomes externalized in some form of human experience. We sometimes wonder why this year we are no better off than we were last year. It may be that last year we had some lack of wealth, health, morals, position, companionship, and this year that same condition exists. We need go no further than to realize that we have added nothing to our consciousness of Truth than was there before, and therefore nothing could happen to the external. We learn that the external existence is the reflection of our internal awareness.

These statements in the Bible, which really are laws, must become a very part of our being. They must be realized, not merely declared or stated; they must become the very fabric of our being, then we can experience the outward result. What is this Consciousness that becomes a God, or law, unto our experience? We have been tracing this truth through what we know in Scripture to arrive at that which we know is universal Truth.

"Why callest thou me good? There is none good but one, that is God." "I can of mine own self do nothing." "The words that I speak unto you, I speak not of myself, but God that dwelleth in me, he doeth the works." We know that these statements show forth the nothingness of the so-called human identity and the all ness of that part of us which is God — the infinite. That is universal Truth. We must understand Truth to be universal. As an illustration, Let us take what we know is the Golden Rule, common throughout all religions. Jesus said, "Therefore all things whatsoever ye would that men should do to you, do ye even so to them:"

Aristotle, Greek — Isocrates, Athenian orator, 300 B.C. — "What you wish your neighbors to be to you, that be to them."

Confucius, Chinese philosopher, 500 B.C. — "Do not unto another what you would not have him do unto you."

Hillel, Hebrew Rabbi and teacher, 50 B.C. — "Do not to others what you would not like others to do unto you."

Sextus, 450 B.C. — "What you wish your neighbors to be to you, such be to them."

RETURNING GOOD FOR EVIL:

Jesus — "But I say unto you, That ye resist not evil: but whosoever shall smite thee on thy right cheek, turn to him the other also." "Love your enemies, bless them that curse you, do good to them that hate you, and pray for them which despitefully use you, and persecute you;" Forgive "Until seventy times seven."

Buddha, Hindu Savior, 500 B.C. — "Overcome evil with good."

Loatze, Chinese philosopher, 500 B.C. — "Recompense injury with kindness. Return love for great hatred."

Socrates, 300 B.C. — "It is not permitted to return evil for evil."

* * * * * *

The most vital truth in the history of the world is the truth, I AM If that truth had been the truth only about one man, it would have had no value to the world as a Principle, but would have merely set up another man to worship. Moses founded his forty year journey with the words, "I AM THAT I AM." It was a sacred moment in his experience when he realized that I AM. Isaiah tells us the same thing when he says, "Before me there are no other gods."

There is only one substance, and that is Mind, and that is universal, and that Mind, that substance, I AM. Out of the Consciousness that I AM is formed my universe, and that is as true of you as it is of me. This Truth that is so universal, this Truth that is the wisdom of the ages, this is the Truth that I AM — not some truth that we are going to learn — not some truth that we are going to find in books. Unless we say that I AM that Truth, we are missing the path, as it has been missed for thousands of years by those who took these teachings and embroidered them.

Chapter 11
Basis of Understanding

"My kingdom is not of this world."

"Cease ye from man whose breath is in his nostrils."

"God is no respecter of persons."

Here we leave behind old landmarks, but whether we will be glad to see them disappear depends on how firmly we grasp the new idea.

We start out from a well-known city — a familiar state of consciousness. We know where we are — we know well the routine of affirmations, denials, formulas, set prayers given us by others to memorize and repeat.

In our present state of unfolding consciousness we have lots of props upon which to lean. We can always fall back upon statements uttered by wise men of old and newer ones by men and women of our own time. We can even call upon that ancient cliché in times of trouble, "Leave it to God." There are well worn prayers and statements in the Bible; there are well known prayers and formulas in modern metaphysical writings. Yes, our present state of consciousness gives us much on which to lean.

When, however, as now, we agree to *leave* old landmarks, we enter a state of consciousness with but few guide posts and even fewer aids. In this new land you will find yourself much alone with God. It will become necessary to make your direct contact with infinite Being — with the infinity of your own being. It will no longer help you to talk about God, pray up to God, lean on God, think about God; now you must become one with God; you must consciously "feel" your oneness and receive direct illumination, guidance.

At first when you close your eyes in silence, there may be a sinking feeling in the pit of the stomach as you realize that here you are — at last — alone with God and God nowhere yet in sight or hearing. It may be like swimming in an ocean and all of a sudden realizing that you have gone out of sight of land with no guide post to tell you which direction to head for.

The first experience when you turn into the silence without words, thoughts or statements, can be very confusing and doubt engendering. It will require patience and perseverance, just as it did in those pioneers who broke through the material wilderness to make first a path from the Atlantic Ocean to the Pacific, and then fill in that path with towns and cities, and finally unfold a great America — a completely new and different country from any before known.

The early pioneers in mental healing found that they could convey the idea of health from practitioner to patient with words silently spoken and with no physical contact between patient and practitioner. The method then was to orally or silently address the patient by name and then orally or silently declare the truth of being through affirmation and denial; and the patient, if at all receptive, was healed or helped.

With the passing of time and much experience, progress in this healing method continued until it arrived at a point where it was no longer necessary to address the patient at all. The practitioner could "know the truth" within himself, and the one who had asked for help would receive it. This was called impersonal treatment. At first it was used only to help those who had not specifically asked for help, but later it was found to be a more efficacious method than directly addressing the mentality of the patient. While all metaphysical practitioners have not advanced to the place where they can heal without directly addressing the patient, the best and busiest practitioners have learned this secret. By the time they reach the place in consciousness where they merely "know the truth" within themselves — or "clear their own thought," as it is sometimes called, they have also arrived at a place where most of their healing work is no longer mental healing, but spiritual healing. The continuous living in the mental realm, leads us to the higher atmosphere of Spirit or Soul. Having arrived at the state of consciousness where the patient is not recognized, is not taken into the treatment, the practitioner has become aware of a divine Presence, Power or Influence within his own being. Instead of his giving mental treatments, he finds this sweet Presence within himself as the divine agent in the healing work. More and more he becomes aware of God as a very present Reality; he "feels" this gentle Presence within; he learns to be consciously aware of it more and more. He, the practitioner, becomes less and less, and God, the divine Within, becomes more and more. There is less faith in statements, thoughts, affirmations and more understanding of God as the Life and substance of the real universe. The errors of the senses are more easily seen as illusion. Less and less effort is given to overcoming sin, healing disease, removing error, or battling mortal mind, or protecting oneself from imaginary powers and evil people. The spiritual Consciousness reveals the physical world as a mirage — an illusion without substance, law, reality, cause or effect. And this spiritual sense dissolves the illusion without mental effort — without prayer or treatment. Just as the enlightened mathematical sense sees 12 x 12 as 144 without "taking thought," without mental strain, effort or process. It just knows 144 — complete and perfect. As this spiritual awareness becomes more and more, the mental work — the mental treatment — becomes less and less. What need is there to strive, struggle, contend and do mental battle with what is now so clearly seen and understood as mirage — nothingness? "My kingdom is not of this world." "Cease ye from man whose breath is in his nostrils." "God is no respecter of persons."

"My kingdom is not of this world." "My kingdom" means the realm of Spirit, Soul, or I AM; "this world" means the universe of concepts; the illusion or mirage. It naturally follows that this means there is nothing of "My kingdom," of the Godly in "this world" — the universe we see, hear, taste, touch or smell.

To you and to me, this is the most tremendous revelation in the Bible. It shows us why there are wars with all their horrors of disaster, wreck, ruin, wounds, insanity, death and destruction — and God does nothing about it. The Second World War ended in Germany only when the Germans were completely and utterly defeated — out of food, clothing and ammunition. Did God stop it then? No. It stopped only because there was nothing with which the Germans could carry on. Did the war in the East stop then? Did God decide to stop the whole war? No. The Asiatic War went on until two atomic bombs — not God — showed the Japanese the hopelessness of their situation. Please remember, shocking as this may seem to you, there was no God on the battlefields; there was no God in the war. Were there only bad men, evil characters and sinful people hurt and destroyed in the war? You know better. Most of the people — even most Germans and Japanese — were good humans, innocent of any desire to hurt anyone. Was God with them? Think of the tornadoes, train wrecks, air casualties. Where is God? God does not enter the human scene So then, what is your function and what is your hope?

You must see and understand "this world" as a mirage, an illusion, a mesmeric suggestion and not attempt to heal it, pray for it, save it or redeem it; but see it for what it is — a false concept of Reality, a dream-picture. When we awaken from this dream world, we will "see Him as He is," and we will then be satisfied that all is well and will "be like Him" — spiritual and perfect. Must we die to awaken to this Truth? No. We must know, understand and acknowledge that what we behold is not the world of Reality, and God is not in it; but seeing through it we behold "the temple not made with hands" — the spiritual universe here and now. What is your hope? That you may live always in the consciousness of "My kingdom," in which is no mortal sense to be overcome, no erring conditions to be corrected, no sinful or sick people to heal.

Looking back, you can realize now how much of your metaphysical work has been in the realm of human betterment. At this moment you are being led to "My kingdom" — to that place or point in consciousness, or that state of consciousness, where harmony is the ever-present and only state of being. Your study, your work, now is no longer for the purpose of ending a war or changing capitalism from socialism. Your endeavor now is to cease from consideration of the things of "this world," so as to tune in on the beam that leads to the realization of "My kingdom."

In God Consciousness there are riches of the Soul, palaces **of spiritual** substance, an existence of eternal bliss. These are not found in material sense, **regardless** of how great and good.

Is this practical in our experience here and now? Let your own **heart** answer. Unless you perceive this with your own inner conviction, my statements or assurances will be meaningless. If my words find a response within you, then you need no further assurance. Trust your instinct, your intuition — *not* as to whether my message is true *(I know it is)*, but as to your readiness for it.

Is there something of "this world" very important to you? Whatever of good there is — and this is infinite — will unfold to you and for you without your taking thought; and it will appear as person, place and thing, but it really will be God appearing, good unfolding, Life expressing, Love revealing.

Do not fear to let go the things and events of "this world." More and better harmonies will appear than ever you dreamed of — and without planning or effort or struggle. And these will still appear in tangible and substantial form — as person, place, and thing — but you will smile and know better; you will recognize them as gifts of God — as divine Grace — as your heritage as the child of God.

Chapter 12
Treatment

No one has a personal message. There is no such thing as a messenger of God. God is His own messenger and He appears to human consciousness at that moment's demonstration. He has appeared as many great thinkers and always in the way that you, as a human person, can comprehend.

Every one of us, whether in the business or professional world or any of the arts is trusted with a doctrine not our own. Originality of ideas is not ours; it is God, individual Mind. There is a fullness and completeness awaiting each person. We are here as the presence of God, fulfilling God's destiny. Every one is an individualization of the infinity of God.

No one can be without opportunity. One of the greatest lessons in this connection is found in the Bible, I Kings 19. Elijah, the only prophet not slain, has fled for his life and is hiding in a cave. The hopelessness of the situation seems to overwhelm Elijah. Here he is the only prophet of God left; his people have forsaken the covenant and have thrown down the altars. To Elijah there certainly seemed to be no opportunity left for him but to die. But in turning to God, what were his instructions? "Go, return on thy way . . . I have left me seven thousand in Israel, all the knees which have not bowed unto Baal, and every mouth which hath not kissed him." So it is with each one of us. There is never a lack of opportunity when it is seen as God's opportunity of presenting Himself to the "seven thousand" that He has saved out for Himself. Then there is no need for envy, jealousy, rivalry or competition, because there is infinity of good which God has saved out for Himself. The moment you present God, the audience is universal.

We learn to let good, let Mind, assume its responsibilities. As we learn to listen for that still, small voice, we, too, will be led to where our work, recognition and compensation are to be found. Cultivate the consciousness of the presence of God every moment.

Until you begin to see God in every form everywhere, you are seeing something apart from God. "The man that I see is the man that I be." The universe returns to us our concepts as we express them. As long as we see error as externalized condition, we fight it, but when we see it as illusion, we get rid of it — it disappears.

Regardless of who asks for help, or what the nature of the claim, the first thing to remember is that your realization has nothing to do with a person, place or thing "out there;" but you are being tempted to accept a person or condition apart from God's own being.

When the call comes for help, immediately recognize that you are being tempted to accept a selfhood apart from God, or a condition unlike good, therefore, you must now work with yourself. You must accept yourself as the patient and you must heal yourself of the belief of a selfhood or condition apart from God. You must accept yourself as the patient and or condition apart from God. You must realize that the entire human scene, good or evil, is the finite sense of Reality. You are not being called upon to separate tracks, even though they appear to come together; you are not be called upon to lift the sky off the mountain, even though the sky appears to be sitting there. You are to realize that sin, disease, lack, even death, is a mirage. And, no mirage ever wets the dry sands of the desert.

Do not ask your patient to do anything for the purpose of helping to heal him. The patient is the very presence of God, all the time and when we recognize that we are being presented with the illusion of sickness or sin, that we are not trying to heal some one or save some one, then right from the first moment we are recognizing that there is only the presence of God, and that what is coming to us as suggestion is only illusion.

You defeat your own realization if you go outside your own consciousness for help. You may recommend any book, pamphlet, lecture, or other reading, for the inspiration it gives, or for the knowledge of Truth it imparts, but never claim that any of these will help in healing. Never discourage or urge prayers attendance or membership. Each one must work out his own salvation at the point of consciousness where he finds himself. Your healing work is done within your own being and is not dependent on what the so-called patient does or thinks.

Be free in imparting Truth to those eager for it and who are capable of listening. Never permit discussion or argument — never try to convince. If the friend, seeker, or patient cannot quickly listen and accept, stop at once. This does not mean that we cannot answer questions — we are eager to do that — but one will not argue, discuss, or try to convince. Just as receptivity is your greatest spiritual quality, so must it be in those who come to you.

How much treating should you do in any case? When you "feel" within you that the work is done, you will not be able to do more, and you will "stand'" in your treatment. Be guided by your inner feelings. If you are keeping your consciousness clear, you will often give no further treatment beyond assuring the patient that you will help immediately. You will intuitively know whether anything further is necessary. Never promise to help later or at any specific time, but always immediately. The "I" of you is a present help to any situation. Even if you cannot stop to do anything further, you can instantly know that no healing is to be done — all is — I AM — nothing in the future can be accomplished. Healing is not something you are going to do — healing is the realization of perfection now — the "feel" of God within you. The demand for help is never on the personal you, but on the I THAT I AM, which is likewise the "I" of the so-called patient. That "I" is ever with him, even as it is with you, and you can trust him to the "I" of his own being — the one, universal I THAT I AM.

Prayer is not what goes from the individual to God — but that which comes from God, the universal, to the individual consciousness. Prayer is the Word of God which comes to you in Silence.

All the human thinking you can do will not help anyone in this world — nor will it harm anyone.

What is the relationship between practitioner, patient and God? Unless we have a clear understanding of this, we will have difficulty with healings and with our work for other people. Nothing goes from the practitioner to God or from the practitioner to the patient.

God, practitioner and patient are all one. If they were not, there would be mediation, intercession, a finite and the infinite. There is one, God. Whenever we are tempted to think that we are something less than God, we are insulting God, or throwing dust in the face of infinity.

The only thing that is taking place in a treatment is the practitioner's realization that all there is present is God; all there is that is power is God. God is appearing as a practitioner, as a patient, but always only one and that one is God. Until the three become one, the treatment is not complete; as long as there is a sense of duality, the treatment is not complete.

Treatment is a realization of God's all ness. There cannot be many, but only one — one appearing as many. We will have the belief in God *and* you as long as we misunderstand this Principle. I AM Life, Soul. My body is its manifestation or expression, but still always one — one as wood and table inseparable and indivisible. Without wood there would be no table.

The only reason for any treatment is a belief in duality. We turn within to re-establish our sense of oneness. We have come into the belief that I and God are two. We must get back to the realization of oneness. If for any reason I seem to be separated from my good health — health —harmony — wealth, the cure is to get back to the Principle of oneness. The reason we lose our sense of oneness is because of a universal sense of mesmerism. All forms of daily life are presenting pictures of good and evil — newspapers, pictures, novels, etc. All of separation, discord, lack. Re-establish the sense of oneness — this is all there is to meditation or treatment.

You will not be successful as long as you are living a dual existence. You must not look for a power outside of yourself. You must not accept the belief that there is an evil power, or look for a good power to act upon you or upon your affairs. You are the law, the Principle of your being and body. The moment you realize that oneness, you have infinity flowing through you. No power outside of you is going to act upon your business, work or demonstration. There is no power sitting around waiting to find you a house to live in, or a job to fill. If there were, it would be a sad world indeed. You, yourself, are the Law, but that law is only law as you realize it within your being — that is, as you get the "feel" of your oneness with God. As a human being, you are not the Law, because if you were, every other human in the world would be, too, and then there would be no discord. If as humans, we were one with the Law, there would be no wars on the earth. But to the contrary, having set up this belief of humanhood, we have set up errors with it.

Treatment is realization and prayer. When realization happens within, the whole outer picture changes. All affirmations are waste motion unless accompanied with realization. You do not have to name the disease or person; you do not have to tell God whether the demonstration is physical, moral or financial; you do not have to voice anything. All you have to do is "be still" — go into the secret place of the most high (your own consciousness) and realize again your oneness with God until a responsive "feeling" comes to you — a sense of awareness. In meditation, everyone's experience is different. That is why we need meditation. Do not, though tell even your best friend about your joys in meditation. It is your secret, your relationship with God, the most sacred relationship in the world, and it should not be shared with anyone. It is yours alone; no one else can really respond to it. True, what blesses one blesses all; but this is a state of consciousness and no two are on just the same level of demonstration. Let fruitage be seen, not talked about. No one has to go around saying he is a millionaire, or that he is joyous and happy; if it can be seen in his walk, his attitude, his clothes. So, to refrain from voicing your experiences in wisdom.

Oneness appears to us as harmony. It is universal Life, one Mind, and this Life is individualized as you. In duality we have health and sickness, abundance and lack, life and death. As long as there is duality, you cannot avoid these opposites. Only in realization of oneness of the divine Life expressing Itself as you, can you look forward to eternal life; only in the realization that you share with God all the heavenly riches, can you know abundance. All of the infinity of God appears *as* you. If it were *in* me, it could possibly find an outlet and get out of me. Therefore, Truth appears *as* me, *as* you. Then when we say, "The kingdom of God is within you," we understand it to mean, that the kingdom is appearing as you.

Otherwise, the infinity of God good, would be finite. This is unfoldment and is universal. It would be selfish if we merely took this home for our own purposes only, or did not use it at all. None of this is intended to increase the amount of truth you know, but all of it is intended as Truth revealing more of God to the world.

There is no limit to what we can do in the realization of our oneness with God. I, of myself, can do nothing, but the moment the demand is made on me and I realize that I am Godly, the limit is lifted. With all of the human good we can express, we can still be slaves. Regardless of how much physical health or wealth we might have, we are still slaves to physical and economic laws until such time as we make the transition from physical sense to spiritual consciousness. In the economic and physical world, we are up against the belief that we are getting old, and so find age a great problem. We do not overcome this until we have advanced beyond just increasing human good, and come to a point of realizing our spiritual identity. There must be a transition from the material sense of existence to spiritual existence. That is the aim and object of all spiritual study.

The reason many spiritual seers and holy men have ended up in poverty or disease is that they always considered there was a God *and* themselves. They were looking to God for something, instead of realizing I AM.

If Life is self-sustained, then why go around worrying, doubting or fearing it. I am Life eternal. A God in heaven does us no good — we must feel it inside. There is no error except the belief in separation from God. Duality is the only devil.

"It is mental quackery to make disease a reality — to hold it as something seen and felt — and then to attempt to cure through Mind." (Science and Health). Mary Baker Eddy's place in history will be based on her revelation of the nature and character of error — that it is illusion, hypnotism, mesmerism. Then we do not have to fight it. Just know it is a mirage, then forget it. "Treat a belief in sickness as you would sin, with sudden dismissal." (Ibid.) Mirage is your belief that what is appearing is other than God appearing. Whatever is appearing can only be God reality itself appearing. The illusion is in the misinterpretation of what is "out there." Illusion is your concept of the manifestation of God; illusion is the belief that it has power to harm. It can't, because it is God appearing and any sense that it is not is the illusion. We must remember that the illusion is not "out there," but only in the misperception of reality itself. Only as we see this, can we begin to see that there is noting and no one to be healed saved or changed.

I exist as consciousness; therefore, nothing comes to me except as consciousness and whatever is in or of my consciousness is good, and I will not be convinced that it is evil.

There is no such thing as personal error. I have no right to condemn or be condemned. Any sense of error is always a universal belief to which I am being subjected. Anything that is universal belief can be overcome or thrown off. Know that you cannot be used as an avenue or channel of expression for these universal beliefs, because only God, good appears as you. This is true of any temptation of form which is a universal claim. We are merely being used as targets or victims. We want to overcome the belief or illusion that there is something there of a nature opposed to God. We then translate the thing into its rightful use. We must realize our oneness with God from the moment we awaken in the morning. Anything in the world can become a poison or injury — that is the way of human belief. Dualism is a very wonderful thing to the human sense. We are breaking down duality. Either there is good and evil, or there is not. But we know that God is the only power; there are no lesser powers; there is no substance apart from God; there is no being apart included in the infinite Godhead. Duality is the only devil we have. "I am the Lord, and there is none else, there is no God beside me:" (Isaiah 45:5).

The Hindu "Aum" and the Biblical "Amen" originally meant," I AM." The very pronouncing was supposed to have healing power.

I already AM, "whither shall I flee from Thy presence?" When the I AM voices itself to us, the human selfhood disappears. Our human hood must not be exalted into thinking it is God.

The "future" is duality and, therefore, is the devil. Any affirmation or denial, written or spoken, that has for its object correcting, improving, healing or getting something is just a waste of time. All any argument is a reminder of that eternal Truth which is now. Right where desire is, manifestation must be.

Now, let us realize the idea of spiritual health, of spiritual joy, of spiritual peace; let us be done with health in the physical realm, or supply of a physical nature, or the material sense of good; let us stop resting in the human sense of good, in the human modes of good. If we do not *now* make the transition into the richer sense of life and health, the healing work cannot take on its highest sense.

The healing of physical conditions is no different when done metaphysically than physically unless it is accomplished through the realization of the spiritual nature of Life, Mind, body harmony, health and dominion. The mental or physical sense of dominion is not our aim. Our purpose is the realization of a spiritual sense of existence and we cannot be satisfied with anything less. The time has come to make the transition from healing matter from healing physical discords, to realization of the spiritual harmony of being — to the spiritual sense of supply — to the spiritual sense of joy and peace and dominion. Joy in the Spirit is an entirely different thing from acquisition of money or fame. The spiritual sense of health is something far beyond a heart beating a normal rate of speed. Eternal Life is not found in the physical realm; neither is infinite supply found in the physical realm, nor the continuous sense of joy or peace or dominion. Therefore, until we rise above this physical sense of existence, we cannot find the eternal or immortal good we are seeking. In the world where human betterment is the rule and the goal, there is also the sense of health and sickness, wealth and poverty — the opposites, in other words — and one may have one today and the other tomorrow. While in the spiritual consciousness of existence, there is only the continuity of good.

Healings now should no longer be a matter of mental power, of mental struggle, of mental striving, of mental effort — healings should be a matter of Grace with you. The time is long past for you to be struggling for a healing; you must have arrived at that state of consciousness in which healings are accomplished through Grace — through Love — with just a smile.

When you understand that only the Mind of you governs and controls your affairs — when you understand that nothing outside of you acts upon you or upon your supply, your health or you body, that everything that is occurring to you is occurring as a direct result of your own state of consciousness, then you can begin to correct whatever is wrong in your affairs in the same way you can become a law unto your affairs and unto all who turn to you for help. You do not have to go through affirmations and denials; you have to cultivate spiritual discernment, and then this spiritual discernment results or acts upon your affairs to bring out harmony and peace and prosperity. In the same way, in proportion as you have a material state of consciousness, in proportion as you believe in matter as real, in that proportion will that material state of consciousness of yours act erroneously and injuriously upon your affairs. To bring out harmony means to spiritualize your thought.

There is that which is invisible to material sense, even invisible to the intellect, but tangible and real to those of inner vision — of spiritual consciousness. It is called the Presence — the Spirit within — and by many other terms. Actually; it is the reality of your being or Inner Self. Its function is to go before you to make the crooked places straight; to be the green pastures and the still water of your existence; to be the Everlasting Arms — the Shadow of the Almighty. It is that which provides manna in the desert; it brings forth water out of the rocks; it closes the mouths of lions; it makes the burning flames of no power; it is the intelligence of your being; it provides for you and in you the answer to every problem. Having recourse to this Inner Presence you are eternally and intelligently governed and sustained regardless of human conditions. Without it you are as a cork on the ocean buffeted by every breeze and every wavelet. With it, you are the wave upheld by the ocean itself, empowered by all the energy of the sea of Life. Without it you are the victim of circumstance and person. With it, you are the captain of your own soul, master of your destiny.

Material sense will never reveal the permanent harmony of being. Intuition is the spiritual faculty — is the spiritual quality. We develop this spiritual sense as we learn to put off the old man who judges by appearance and gain the new man who intuitively perceives the reality behind the mask of personality. Those who do not yet know the Inner Self wear the mask of self-protection, self-importance, self defense — only until they learn that God is their real Being and needs no artificial aids.

Men steal because they do not know that they embody their good, they carry Bibles with steel linings because they do not know that the Word is their sufficient protection. They protect the Word itself with steel plates. This is tragic, and sometimes we too try to protect ourselves with words and statements, instead of knowing that the Word itself in Silence is our very Life.

Chapter 13
Infinite Individual Consciousness

Every individual in the world has within his own consciousness every invention, every art that was ever known. We are the embodiment of every law in the universe. Through a process that we call learning we seem to be taking in a little metaphysics today, a little music tomorrow, while the truth is they are already a part of our consciousness, our awareness of them is only unfolding by degrees. There are people who are able to grasp these things without going through the usual process. This is cosmic Consciousness. This explains child prodigies. These people are universal Mind without any obstruction. The closer we get to the realization of this universal Consciousness, the more infinitude becomes apparent. Truth is not added to your consciousness — it comes through unfoldment. Our so-called human Consciousness is a shutter. At one point, it admits very little light; opened a little more, it admits more light, and as we become more and more spiritually minded, the shutter opens wider and wider, until eventually all human hood disappears. The full light then shines through.

We cannot increase our consciousness, it is infinite already, but we can become aware of its infinite nature. You cannot add to yourself; you cannot even become more spiritual or more wise, but only more aware of the infinity of your own spiritual consciousness, in proportion as you realize that God is the Mind, substance and Spirit of you.

We may come to the study of metaphysics or the Bible to gain better health; or we may come to the search for God to increase our wealth or business activity, but in the last analysis that is not what is going to happen to us. True, this increased sense of spiritual good will produce better human hood, increase our ease in matter, and even prolong our human sense of existence a few years, but this is not the object of our study. The object of our search for Truth is to gain a spiritual sense of existence that we may live perfectly and eternally.

We may suddenly find that the particular disease or discord or lack has disappeared, but this is of value only if it serves as a steppingstone to the real demonstration of spiritual existence. If it does not lead to this, at best it can only be a case of exchanging a bad piece of body for a good piece of body. The average student of metaphysics is satisfied to stop right there and let life become just one round of demonstrations, or attempted ones. Truth becomes just a new form of medicine to him. The effect is just the same as calling a doctor to administer a pill and the real error is not handled. Truth is not supposed to heal me, but to reveal to me the spiritual nature of my being so that I do not need a constant round of treatments.

We also turn to the study of the Bible to experience that better sense of companionship in a friend, husband, wife or child.

The purpose of our study then is, first, the improvement of our human hood — the improvement in our human existence, in health, wealth, harmony, companionship — but, let us not stop there.

In seven thousand years of recorded history, we have never had peace in the world and this in spite of all the thousands of religions that are on the earth. All of these have failed to bring about the condition of peace — and for one reason: they have failed to emphasize the oneness of the individual and God. When we realize this oneness we realize this is the true relationship in the world. There is no longer any need for war. In the realization of oneness, we demonstrate the impossibility of racial or religious prejudice or the envying of anyone's possessions. This knowledge is useable; these things are absolutely demonstrable laws of the Bible, laws of Being and will wipe out bigotry, desire for another's possessions, prejudice. It is impossible to hate or fear anyone after the attainment of the realization of oneness. After the moment of realization we do not need places of worship, books or ministers. Spiritualized man is the only thing we need to realize.

Life is self-sustained. What life? The only life we have —your Life, my Life. It has no need for anyone to give it a lift. This great vision will come to us only when we transcend human hood and begin to live the divinity of our Being.

Quotations from the Bible are meaningless while they are in the realm of quotations, but when we accept them as laws, then they become laws unto our demonstration. "Ye are the light of the world." Accepted, this statement becomes a law unto our demonstration.

From the earliest Bible readings, mention is made of the "coming of the Messiah." This promise taken literally is meaningless; it can do nothing for us The only value of the prophecy of the coming of the Messiah will be when it is understood to be the coming of the Messiah in your consciousness and in my consciousness, and we must awaken to the realization that we are that spiritual man —the Messiah — the one called Peace, Mighty Counselor. If the historical sense of the Bible is literally true, , during the time when the Messiah was promised, would have been years of absolute darkness — without a Messiah of any kind. If we now accept that we are Godly, and "Before Abraham was, I am," then we find there has always been a Messiah in the world. Therefore, these promises can have no bearing on the facts, and these statements must have some other vital significance.

The coming of Messiah is the coming of perfection in you and in me — not the coming of a man who would be perfect. We are born as humans, seemingly, and we grow up as humans. Through study we do develop some degree of Universal Consciousness, but we learn that that is not enough. We have to develop this Consciousness to a greater degree: attending prayers, reading the Bible or metaphysical writings, and to the degree that we have utilized these helps, we are making progress or we have slipped up. We should utilize as much as possible the line of thought laid down for morning work in the Chapter, "Meditation" in The Infinite Way. The purpose of this is the realization of our oneness with God. In this manner we cultivate the spiritual senses and awaken consciousness to divine Reality.

It is only the belief that we are human beings that is separating us from our good at this very moment. The only antidote for it is the truth that "I and God are one." But just reciting this statement will do no good. Statements of truth are what you read in books and hear from men, but Truth itself is what you discern between the lines. Any affirmation can only be a statement about Truth, not a truth itself. However, it can serve to keep you in line with the infinite until consciousness responds and opens up. Therefore, it should be our conscious work to realize our oneness with God and with every spiritual idea. This does not mean with every human being in the world, but literally with the idea of happiness, prosperity, friendliness, health. When we realize our oneness with these qualities, we demonstrate them. This realization not only enables us to express these qualities to others, but compels others to express them to us.

The Bible should never be considered personal, not even when it uses names of people, places, cities, or rivers, but significant of spiritual qualities, spiritual activities. One who is awaiting the coming of the Messiah, are putting off their hope of salvation to some future time. This is fatal to demonstration. Supposing for some reason we found ourselves out in the street, all property, possessions etc. gone; we have nothing behind us to turn to; we are entirely alone. Is God any less God at that moment than the moment before when we thought we had so much? This is a point we must understand. What is this Messiah? Your Consciousness — the infinite, divine spiritual Consciousness which is your individual consciousness when its sense of a power apart from God has been overcome. So then, if you sat perfectly still without a thought except "Thank you God, there I am" and "Where I am, God is" — not two, but one — you would soon find yourself in a very short period of adjustment, on the very same level of supply and health that you had before the loss. As your consciousness unfolds, it will maintain and support you on the same level which you have already attained.

In the human thought there are states and stages of consciousness and when the personal I, or ego, is paramount, we are mostly in the getting end of life —achieving, accomplishing, acquiring — all our life is directed towards coming in to us — while the highest state of humanhood is marked by the concern for helping, teaching, co-operating then life is flowing out from us, and we are more concerned with helping and sharing than we are with getting. In the spiritual life, we go higher than that — we are the Light of the world — and we are no longer concerned about who comes into our orbit, how many, or if there are none at all. Our concern then is really being the Light of the world — showing forth the greater harmony of spiritual existence and allowing that harmony and perfection in us to attract those who are seeking something better than they already have.

God has no favorites; therefore, a spiritual sense is not concerned with helping and teaching the other fellow. It stands, rather, like the lighthouse, waiting for the other fellow to awaken himself to his own identity. I am only a Light of the world in proportion as I realize that there is no darkness in the world, and any appearance to the contrary is illusion. This is where our metaphysical work begins. We must live in the consciousness that we as individuals are the Light of the world, and because we do not come down from that point, that high estate, those not yet awakened to their true identity find, through their contact with us, that they, too are the Light of the world.

The consciousness of the individual is the Messiah, and when we arrive at that understanding, we realize that there is no need for recognition or reward. The promise of the coming of the Messiah is the promise of the coming to our individual awareness that the Messiah that is already within — that was there before Abraham — that will be there until the end of the human sense of the world — until there is no longer need for this great Light to be sifted down through a shutter.

The amount of daily work done in meditation determines the amount of unfoldment, and that, in turn, determines the amount of outer demonstration.

You will never get rid of your body, but you will get rid of the false, material, sense of your body. Life should become an adventure — not a Social Security number.

Chapter 14
Oneness

Spiritual Interpretation of Scripture reveals that there is but one God, one Power, one Presence — and that one good; Than evil, therefore, can exist only as illusion or mirage. It further reveals that that God, Presence, Power, is not something separate or apart from me, but rather is the reality and substance of my very being." "I am He." Viewing Niagara Falls from the front, we wonder that it does not run dry. Seeing it from another direction, we see behind Niagara Falls the great Lake Erie. Now we realize that Niagara is but a name given to Lake Erie where the great lake tumbles over the Falls. What appears as Niagara is really Lake Erie at the place of the Falls; thus Niagara Falls and Lake Erie are really one and not two.

"I and God are one." I am that place where God becomes individualized and evident as me. Emerson shows forth his recognition of this Truth in the first paragraph of his Essay, "History": "There is one mind common to all individual men. Every man is an inlet to the same and to all of the same. He that is once admitted to the right of reason is made a free man of the whole estate. What Plato has thought, he may think; what a Saint has felt, he may feel; what at any time has befallen any man, he can understand. Who hath access to this universal mind is a part to all that is or can be done, for this is the only and sovereign agent."

Deep within your inner being there is an invisible Presence which has been felt by the prophets and seers of all ages. Moses felt it in his bosom when shepherding on the hills. Elijah and Elisha communed with it within themselves and performed miracles. It gave power and vision to Isaiah and Jeremiah, Joel, Jacob and all the line of Hebrew leaders. Every man has this divine Presence deep within himself. Without it you would be a piece of dead flesh; with it you are a living reasoning, loving being.

Open your Bible and turn to some of the stirring stories of David, Solomon, Joseph, Samuel and other prophets, and think of the spirit within them; the spirit of Love that moved them to perform great deeds for their people; the spirit of Truth which urged them on to serve the weak, the poor and the suffering. This same Spirit is within you. It forms *your* desire to live, to serve, to succeed.

This spirit dwells in you, awaiting only your recognition and acceptance. It is a giant power house within you just requiring a touch to make it break forth with dynamic energy to build your life and body anew.

YESTERDAY'S MANNA:

We do not "Live by bread alone," but by the Word of God which comes to us from within our own being. Our daily joy is in turning in silence to that center with us and learning to hear "The still, small voice." Nor need we live on yesterday's manna. There is no time in the world when the sustaining Word is not awaiting us. There is no day when we cannot turn and attune ourselves to the Kingdom within and receive the guidance, encouragement, wisdom and supply needed at that moment. We do not have to live on yesterday's manna. Even yesterday's money, fame or friends are not necessary because the Presence within us feeds us daily with fresh manna as we learn to receive it. Neither gloat nor mourn over yesterday's manna. Today is your day to receive it afresh.

SPIRITUAL INTERPRETATION OF BIBLE LAWS:

Law of Tithing: Tithing, giving a percentage of one's income to charitable or spiritual purposes, must be understood as an act of gratitude, not as a law of expectation for some good in the future. When tithing is indulged in with any sense of a future tense, it is no longer tithing, but bribery. When tithing is an expression of gratitude, then it is a law of good.

Law of Praying for One's Enemies: You must first of all rise to the spiritual sense of life and thereby realize that harmony, success, peace and freedom are not achieved at the expense of another. As you understand that "The place whereon I stand is holy ground." So must you realize for the entire spiritual universe that the entire universe is spiritual, perfect and free. To hold any person, race, religion, group or nationality as inferior, as enemies, is to deny the Truth, and no prayer is then of any avail. You must study the passages in scripture which symbolize this teaching of praying for one's enemies and live it thoroughly.

Chapter 15
Prayer

Shall I tell you why there is so much lack of demonstration in metaphysical circles? It is because there is a dependence on statements of Truth — affirmations and denials —instead of an effort to make an actual contact or realization of God-being. Talking about God — Truth — wholeness —health will not do. Talk less. Pray more. What is prayer? Is it some word or message *you* send to God? No. Prayer is the Word of God which comes to you when you are silent enough, still enough, expectant enough to receive it. This Word of God which you receive in Silence becomes visible as health, harmony, success, peace, joy and dominion where all the world may see it.

Until every one of us can report that we receive the Word of God continuously, that we can almost at will feel the divine Presence, there will be need of these reminders. From this point on, there is very little need of our learning more Truth. You already know what God is; what the Messiah is; what man is; and you know the nature of error and how it claims to operate. At least you can pass an oral or written examination on these subjects and get no less than 100 per cent. Every one of us is intellectually clear on these major points of metaphysics. If any of you doubt your complete understanding of these metaphysical truths, then hurry up and get yourself letter perfect in them: God —Messiah — man — error.

The next step is prayer, or treatment. I prefer to think of treatment as a conscious realization, through argument, of the truth about God, Messiah, man and error; and prayer as the spiritual consciousness of Truth through Silence. In other words, treatment would deal with the letter, or argument, leading up to realization, and prayer would be the pure Silence and receptivity to the spiritual consciousness of harmony. You understand, of course, that ordinarily in metaphysics treatment and prayer are synonymous, but that I have made this distinction for myself.

To me, prayer is a state of receptivity in which Truth is realized without taking conscious thought. At first prayer is best practiced when sitting quietly and peacefully in harmonious surroundings. We are more apt to achieve Silence when we are away from disturbing noises and unsympathetic thoughts. I mean by this, when we are not in the same room with people who do not understand or lean toward our thought., we should find meditation or prayer an easy matter when we are together like this. We have the stillness of night and the companionship of each other — all of us are eager for this experience of God-consciousness. The Pentecostal experience comes easily when we are together — in one place and of one Mind. As we continue our daily praying — setting aside three or four periods each day and extending to greater length at least the morning and evening periods — the attainment of Silent Receptivity becomes more and more natural and simple.

Gradually we find ourselves in prayer while at work —driving — walking. Ultimately we achieve it even while conversing or while in a room where much talk goes on —even while at the theatre and movies in the very midst of the performance. It all begins with practicing the listening ear. Learn to keep that right ear half cocked all the time. Never get so engrossed in what you are doing that you forget the listening ear. Do not be concerned with or about results. We have no more right to think about results than the beginner at the piano should be thinking of playing a concert. Constant receptivity to the Inner Self should be our aim.

I have shown you in Scripture authority for the teaching that I AM. You followed the revelation of the Orientals in the many statements that I AM; you heard Moses declare, "I AM THAT I AM."

Likewise, I gave you unstinted authority for my unfoldment of the nature of error. It would be a truth and a correct teaching if I had given you no authority but my word — but never have I presented anything to you as wholly original because I have found authority all through the ages of history for what has also revealed itself to me. Having satisfied you that I am offering nothing new, except perhaps an individual manner of presentation, I feel that you should be ready to judge anything now on the strength of your own reaction to it. In other words, by now you should be sufficiently consciously aware of the one Mind to be able to read or hear any statement of metaphysics and know for yourself whether or not it is a truth or personal belief.

I want to introduce to you a most radical teaching — and frankly, I would not dare do it even to you advanced students unless I could gently carry you across a bridge of authority. Even this bridge will not make the teaching less radical — but it will serve to hold you up until you have demonstrated it in some measure.

While presenting to you the revelation of your true identity as infinite spiritual Consciousness, I, nevertheless, kept you in familiar surroundings so that the jump would not be too great. But we are now starting out on a voyage into what may be deep waters; and you will need to remind yourselves often that the one Mind is your only Mind, and, therefore, you can depend on IT for guidance and direction and protection.

Have you ever thought about how you would heal if you could not use the human mind?

Chapter 16
Cleansing the Temple

When you come to the realization of God within you, come with a sincere desire to be cleansed within. You are not merely coming to a teaching from which you expect to receive more or better human conditions. You are not merely seeking to have your human existence made easier, healthier or even a bit longer — but you really are asking to be lifted entirely above the human level of life to an awareness and demonstration of Life eternal — the spiritual consciousness of Life and its harmonies. Do not then hold on to the personal sense of good that has so long obstructed your vision of the Messiah. Be willing; be prepared for God to dispel all personal sense — even that which is humanly good. To come to this realization, and yet consciously insist on holding on to greed, hate, envy, lust, bigotry, jealousy and ingratitude — is to invite disaster.

When you open your thought to the Messiah with honesty, the divine Presence will dispel all erroneous traits and characteristics, and will reveal you as the perfect spiritual Temple.

If you cling to certain errors while inviting the entrance of the Messiah into the Temple of your being, you set up a warfare between the Spirit and the flesh — between the Soul and material sense — and this warfare may wreck the Temple of your being, your body, at least temporarily. Come to this search for Truth with spiritual integrity. Your present sins, faults and limitations are not to be feared. They will disappear as you surrender the personal or material sense of existence for the spiritual consciousness of Life.

The Metaphysical Dictionary says, "Solomon's Temple is a symbol of the regenerated body of man, which, when he attains it, he will never again leave. This enduring Temple is built in the understanding of Spirit as the one and only cause of all things."

When you realize God, as the only causative Principle, you likewise understand that all that exists is of that eternal substance and is therefore immortal. This understanding constitutes your spiritual awareness of Life and its formations, and when you have achieved this understanding, you will never lose your supply or your body, you will have attained eternal Life here and now and there will be no more death or passing, or even disease, for you.

In building this new consciousness you are building the Temple "not made with hands, eternal in the heavens." This Temple you cannot build with materials other than the pure substance of Spirit. You cannot build with human qualities of evil, nor even with human qualities of good. You cannot build it with wrong thinking, but no more can you build it with right thinking. Human thought will not build this infinite eternal spiritual edifice. Human thought is finite and changeable, and it cannot result in an indestructible and immortal structure.

The Temple of God which is your body, and which is also the body of all that concerns your individual existence, is not visible to "man whose breath is in his nostrils." The real body, or Temple of your existence, is seen only with spiritual vision, even as it is built and maintained only by spiritual consciousness.

You do not have to declare that you have attained this consciousness, it is evident even to the world by the harmonies, joys, peace and dominion you show forth in daily living. Your spiritual attainment is evident by its effects which are seen as health, success, poise and peace. Even that which the world sees as your physical body will be apparent as health, vitality, youthfulness and beauty. That which the world sees as your supply will be evident as abundance and security. That which the world sees as your home will reflect love, compatibility, companionship. In other words, that which you receive in secret, in Spiritual Consciousness, will be shouted from the housetops as visible evidence — and yet you will utter no word with your mouth.

Again the Bible Dictionary says, "Spiritual thought and spiritual meditations are constantly carrying us to the place of ascension where form is resolved into its divine idea." By consecration of thought to spiritual ideals, or by meditation, we attain this state of consciousness wherein we find our perfect and immortal existence. By listening we attain a state of receptivity, through which all the Realities are revealed to us. In this consciousness we do not live by bread alone, nor do we live by taking thought; instead life to us becomes a state of Grace — the very gift of God. Let us begin first with the concept of God, Teacher and Practitioner. At first we look to a God somewhere in the sky — or at least Something apart from our self; then, as we seek, we begin to feel God near or with us. Finally we realize God as the Reality or Soul of our very being. Then we understand that there is no separation between God and ourselves, that we are one — and in that oneness we find completeness, perfection, harmony and Grace. With our Teacher — it follows the same pattern: at first we seek teaching from a book; it may be a Bible, a textbook of metaphysics, a lecture or sermon. We then go further and feel the need of a Teacher in living form, a man or woman external to ourselves. The book serves to raise consciousness to where it seeks a higher form of Teacher — and this translates itself to us as a man or woman teacher. This Teacher acts to raise our consciousness still higher to the level where we apprehend that all the while we were seeing Teacher as a book or man, we were actually being taught by God, our divine Consciousness appearing outwardly (because we were seeking outwardly) as man or book. If the book and the man were true, they have led us gently to the Kingdom of our own being, where we behold the Teacher within and thus realize that what appeared as a Teacher outside was actually our own consciousness appearing. There is no higher revelation than this, because the Teacher has led you to the realization of the infinity of your own being, embracing and including the Teacher and the Teaching — Truth itself.

We are going through the fire of human experience and each time we come together in silent receptivity, that other One enters our united consciousness and that divine Presence becomes, a vital Influence for all time. Once realized, the Spirit of God is never lost. We would feel naked if we ever again faced the world without this Presence before us and behind us and beside us. Once realized, this Love becomes the essence or substance of all our experiences. What we behold "out there" is but the shadow cast by the Reality which fills our being.

We come now to spiritual healing, or healing without mental argument. Who and what is the Practitioner? In seeking help we at first sought a man or a woman we believed to be more spiritual than ourselves. We did not realize that that man or woman was our concept of the healing The Messiah was really a divine idea within us, within our consciousness. Do you see whither we are going? What you have believed to be a man or woman "out there," is the Messiah, the healing Influence within you. Now let us go another step. You are the Practitioner on whom one has called for help or healing. You now know that the human sense of you is not a Practitioner, but that of you which is Practitioner is really the Messiah of the so-called patient. Now what have you to say or argue or treat? What necessity is there for mental argument if you have caught the truth about God —Teacher Practitioner — the Truth of Oneness?

Chapter 17
Unveiling the Messiah

I find it necessary to repeat that you will make no headway spiritually until you acknowledge that the Mind of you is the only law unto your affairs. There is nothing outside or apart from you acting upon your health or body. If there is a discord in, or harmony, you yourself must realize that the mesmerism of sense cannot use you as a target or victim. True, the error of sense is not personal; it is not you who are the sinner or wrong thinker — yet it is you who are accepting some suggestion, which in turn is manifesting as sin or fear or disease. Sometimes evil comes to us in the guise of good.

Assuming the troubles and burdens of others is one beautiful way to let in discords. Our task should be the realization of the freedom of everyone — even those who appear outwardly in bondage to sense. To sympathize or pity them is to accept the conditions as real, and this opens our thoughts to many errors. In one way or another you are accepting the suggestion of error — and usually it is through some form of human love or hate.

Wake up. I mean wake up this minute. See your human love or hate as mesmeric suggestion. See it for what it is and stop being handled by it. Stop your sympathy and pity for the embattled Greeks or the starving Armenians or the persecuted Jews. This will not make you hardhearted, but it will enable you to pierce the veil of illusion and thus help the receptive thought. Your sympathy will only fasten the condition more firmly in thought. If you pity your patient, you will not heal him. "Loose him and let him go" — or can't you do that?

In philosophy there is the law of cause and effect; in Oriental philosophy it is known as Karma, or payment for sins and rewards for good. Karma is the philosopher's law of cause and effect. If this is all true, the chaos of today will not be settled by human agreements, nor by prayers to God to set aside the laws of Scripture. One way alone is open. 'Wherefore turn yourselves, and live ye." When the people of the world forego the evil practices of their governments and adopt a policy of equal love to all mankind — only then will individual and national and international harmony appear. There *is* a Messiah within the individual and he must do nothing of himself, but to *let* this inner Presence do all things for him.

You can readily understand that with the actual awareness of an infinite Power and Presence within him one could always count upon It — depend fully upon It — to provide all things, to heal for him, even to feed five thousand when necessary. It is like the fable of having a lamp to rub. But it is not a fable, because the Within knows the need even before it becomes humanly apparent. I suppose that at first we need some measure of faith to believe that there *is* such a thing as this Messiah. No doubt, brought up as we have been, we simply cannot understand that there is more to us than body and thinking capacity. Taught as we have been for so long that we must be "go-getters" — that "the early bird catches the worm" — it must be difficult to realize that there is another Way — spelled with a capital "W" — an infinite Way, or may I rather say, a Way which is infinite, eternal, harmonious, joyful, successful and oh, so real and lasting, leaving no bitterness in the mouth. This infinite Way is the Messiah within us, therefore, I AM the Way — or, the Way is I AM.

Witnessing the great works of Moses, Solomon, Elijah; noting the lasting qualities of the Buddha, Shankara — we must admit they had the conscious awareness of Something more than humanhood. This something is the same Messiah in them, which is also in you. The consciousness of this Presence within makes available to any individual the whole Power and Presence manifested and demonstrated by the Messiah. The Messiah is present within as the Consciousness of everyone of the past ages, of the present and of those still to appear to our sight. There has never been a need for greed, lust, miserliness, hoarding, stealing or marauding — except that men have lost their awareness of this Within. You have It. It is a slumbering Giant in you — or perhaps you are the slumbering one with a very wakeful Giant within — and perhaps this Infinity is kicking so hard at your inner being that it forced you here to awaken to its Presence.

At first glance, this appears to be the solution to your problems and mine only — but right here it becomes necessary for us to realize what change would take place should men and women awaken to this truth.

Perhaps what I have said will make plain to you why there have always been wars, covetousness, false desires, and ambitions. Does this not make the reasons for all the world problems clear to you? Can you not see how inevitable these problems are and will be as long as man believes that he of his own self must provide, achieve, accomplish? As long as man attempts to solve the riddle of supply with human means there will be recourse to the misuse of these powers. The human mind and material force do not contain the answer to universal peace, harmony and prosperity. The realization of the spiritual Light or Presence within is the only permanent solution.

At the moment, the task of realization of the Messiah seems hopeless on any world-wide scale. So few individuals have at any one time had this conscious awareness that it does not seem hopeful that mankind will awaken now in any great numbers. And yet there are signs that this may be taking place. The very depth of the world's need may be driving it awake — or perhaps consciousness has been getting prepared for it since time began through a process of evolution.

First, however, let us admit there *is* an infinite Way and that Way the consciousness of the presence of the Spirit within. Then let us strive, through dwelling on the idea, through meditation, prayer or communion, to attain this consciousness — then live it, teach it, show forth its healing influence so that all receptive to it will open up in its Light and warmth. At this point, I feel that some of you will start checking with yourselves to see if you are living up to the standard of conduct outlined here — and perhaps will believe that your human conduct will advance you spiritually. Now reverse that: as your spiritual nature unfolds, your so-called human conduct improves. Too many already believe that if they can improve their human thoughts and acts, it will bring them closer to the spiritual sense. Reverse that: in proportion as spiritual consciousness becomes more real, the conditions of so-called human existence improve; therefore, do not make the effort to improve your self humanly, but keep your vision on the spiritual and real, and let your so-called human life unfold progressively. One might believe that gaining physical health or wealth is a step towards the spiritual. In that case, exercise and diet would be an aid to spirituality — or a successful business might help. No. "Thou wilt keep him in perfect peace whose mind is stayed on Thee." As you live in a higher consciousness — on a higher plane — your human world so — called will unfold harmoniously, joyfully, peacefully and successfully. For this reason, the exercise of the human thought is not the factor in healing or in being healed. As spiritual Truth reveals itself in your consciousness, the harmony of body or business appears in tangible evidence; therefore, receptivity should be your watchword. It may be tantalizing to be told that the attempted improvement of human thought and conduct is not the basis of spiritual development. We are really trying so hard to be so careful of our thinking and acting. Well — that does no harm; perhaps even that effort is Spirit's way of breaking through. Only be careful — don't stop there. Human goodness is but a way station on the way with a capital "W".

GRACE:

There is an invisible bond between all of us — that is one reason we have been brought together. We are not met together as humans. The aims and motives which govern humans are not in operation here. We are not here to get anything from one another — but to share the spiritual treasures which emanate from God — the Light of our being. Our interest and aim in being here is the unfolding of the Spirit within. We do not look upon each other as man or woman, rich or poor, grand or humble. At least for the hour all human values are submerged in our common interest: to seek and find the Kingdom within. We see each other as fellow-travelers on the Path of Light; we share our unfoldments, our experiences and our spiritual resources. We would not withhold any of these from each other. Of that I am positive and you are too. Likewise, there is no envy or jealousy of each other's spiritual experiences or attainments. Let us even for a moment realize that whatever we have of supply, position, human prestige or power, health, beauty and wealth, is the gift of God and, therefore, available to all of us in the measure of our openness of consciousness — and you can see how we could carry our impersonal love out into the human factors of existence. Let us once catch the vision that whatever anyone possesses, even of what appears to be as human values, is but the expression of a state of consciousness, and it would be as impossible to envy or desire any of the other's possessions or lands as it would be to envy our neighbor his sunshine in the garden.

The first step in living without taking thought — living by Grace — living in universal peace — must begin here and now. Begin with the understanding that we are not humans, but that we are actually Godly; that all that I have is of God, therefore, it is spiritual; that every one of us is Children of God, and we need not labor, strive, struggle or work for that which is divinely ours. You know that no human element has entered this relationship. No one wants or can get anything of a material nature from another; no one has in thought the social or financial position of another; we have but one thing in thought when we gather and that is the unfoldment of our awareness of spiritual Truth and Light.

Now let us stop for a moment and realize this momentous statement: all that any one here possesses, even of a seemingly material nature, is the unfoldment of their own state of consciousness and, therefore, belongs only to the possessor; that what we have or have not is the expression of our individual state of consciousness and we can have as much more as we desire by enlarging the borders of our understanding and realization. Nothing that we could get from another could ever be ours — even if we got it legally; it would still belong only to the one with the consciousness of it. And what is yours is eternally yours and only because it is your state of consciousness in expression. Now — in the name of God — who and what is there to envy, hate, fear or desire? All that God (my very own consciousness) hath — *is* mine. The realization of this Truth would make of us lifelong friends — living without a human fear, lust, greed or any other negative emotion. We would be in a Garden of Eden. This is the first step toward living by Grace — and this is our first recognition of an invisible spiritual tie binding us in an eternal, impersonal brotherhood of Love. By degrees we will extend this vision and the invisible chain.

Chapter 18
The True Sense of the Universe

The beliefs we entertain about the body constitute our sense of body. The truth about body is something entirely different from our concepts of it. The body itself is perfect. It is as immortal and eternal as Soul, God, which is the substance and Principle of the body.

Your body — seen through the universal material beliefs of the world — was born, matures, ages and dies. This very body when correctly known, that is, spiritually discerned, is the very appearing of Soul-substance, Spirit-substance, eternal being. It is neither functional nor organic. What appears to us as functions and organs are our false finite concepts of the activity of Mind appearing as spiritual body or spiritual formation.

As long as we entertain a material concept of body, we will have concern for it — we will cater to it — and find in it both pain and pleasure. As we continue to lift our concept of body until we gain the realization of what our body really is, we will find less and less of either pain or pleasure in it until we arrive at the state of consciousness where we realize the body as an impersonal vehicle or mode of expression.

Every suggestion of discomfort or unharmony coming from the body must be met instantly with the understanding of the true nature of body as spiritual. Only as we understand that errors of sense exist merely as suggestion and false sense, can we find freedom from the pains and pleasures of the body. We are never correcting the body, its so-called organs or functions. We are correcting the false concept or sense of body.

All we have said here about body is equally true about business, home, security, wealth.

There is nothing of God, or reality, in the world we see, hear, taste, touch or smell. The failure of religion in this age is due to the lack of this vision. Theology is attempting to spiritualize a mortal concept of God — called man. This man and his universe is no part of

God, because God or His kingdom is not of this world. Be assured that if God were in this scene there would be no wars, accidents, diseases or deaths. God, the infinite Power of good, is able to maintain harmoniously and eternally Its own creation. In "My kingdom", the realm of Spirit and Truth, there are no errors, no decompositions or defeats.

Prayers uttered for the purpose of healing, improving or aiding the people or conditions of the physical universe, reach no farther than one's own belief and bring only the results of our belief. Any beneficial effects from such prayers are not from God, the universal intelligence and Life, but are the outcome of our faith. Likewise, metaphysical treatment, if it seeks to change the human scene, can only bring forth the fruitage of the confidence placed in the treatment — or faith in the one treating, or else faith in the suppositional God to whom the prayer is addressed.

God is the divine Reality of individual being. To avail oneself of the harmonious government of this Principle, it is necessary to drop all thought of human persons and conditions; lose all desire to improve human hood and *let* the Inner Self reveal in Silence the harmony, wholeness and joy of real Being.

Spiritual good is not composed of more or better material conditions. No amount of increased physical health or wealth can testify to the reign of Spirit or Truth. We rise above sense evidence to find the realm of the real. Soul power — that which we contact within ourselves —results in what appears to be health, harmony and wealth, but these are not the same as that which is attained through attempts to improve the human. The harmony in our affairs which results from our contact with our Inner Self, or Soul, is the manifestation or expression of Spirit, Life; and is the "added things" which come naturally from the realm of real substance. Finite sense beholds these "added things," or spiritual reality, as objectified material sense, or "things" and "persons". Spiritual harmony is not attained by seeking persons, things or conditions, but by taking no thought for these and seeking only contact with the divine Reality of you.

Humans cannot put on or wear the robe of the Messiah. The human mind cannot be spiritualized — it must be "put off." When the Messiah appears as individual spiritual Consciousness, it dispels mortal or material sense. The human is never spiritually "clothed upon" but, as spiritual consciousness appears, material or human sense is dissolved. The effort through mental means to become spiritual is wasted effort. The attempt to understand spiritual things with the five senses or the intellect is useless. Developing a sense of receptivity; learning to silence the senses and gaining the ability to listen for "the still, small voice" — this is the Way. Human thoughts —even good ones — will not help.

So in treatment to close the eyes and declare truths, make affirmations and denials, this is not the way of the Messiah. Be silent — hold a listening attitude, be receptive, be still — and *let* the presence and power of God be made manifest through Silence — this is the Way. The Godly Way is not a transfer of thought from one individual to another; it does not include suggestion or hypnotism. It is a silent state of Receptivity in which the God is manifest as our individual consciousness. It appears principally as a "feeling" of the Presence, and dispels the illusion of sense for oneself or another. As we are touched by the Messiah — as our consciousness becomes more and more the Messiah itself, the receptive consciousness of those asking for help likewise feels this spiritual influence and responds to it and harmony is made evident.

The Messiah does not come down from its high estate to serve or cater to mortals. The Messiah is the Light of the world, and those desirous of its blessings and benefits must leave the husks of material living — must forsake sense satisfaction — even human rights and other forms of human good — and follow Me. There is no place where the human and the spiritual blend. Stay where you spiritually are — high in consciousness — and those who have discovered the nothingness of mortal dreaming — will come to you.

Franz Kafka writes: "You do not need to leave your room. Remain sitting at your table and listen. Do not even listen, simply wait. Do not even wait, be quite still and solitary. The world will freely offer itself to you to be unmasked, it has no choice, it will roll in ecstasy at your feet." This is true of your high estate — your uplifted consciousness. Once you touch or are touched by this, whatever you call then stand and *let* those attracted receive Its benediction. Do not attempt to carry It to humanity — on that path lie unnecessary heartaches and persecutions. Only those ready can comprehend It — and they are seeking you and finding It. Or perhaps more correctly, they are seeking It and finding you. "Give unto him that is athirst" not to those who are finding satisfaction in lesser waters. These feel they are being sated and have no greater desires. Only when intense thirst comes again and again will they realize there is a Water, which when they drink of It, they will never thirst. These are already at the door of your consciousness. Bid them enter.

I want you all to understand the great secret of the universe. Had the ancients known it, our modern living would be as in a paradise. If we learn it in this age, we can help to usher in the Millennium. The few who have known this secret in past ages could not teach it; it would appear that only a very few had the spiritual capacity to grasp its meaning. Some few understood it intellectually, but rarely was it understood in its spiritual significance.

I am not a dreamer of idle dreams — but I have a vision of eternal Life. I would not have you either sitting on a cloud or anchored with your feet on the ground. My idea and my ideal is that you be rooted and grounded in Truth; that you be fed with spiritual meat and that you drink waters from the wellsprings of eternal Spirit and Soul.

The secret — that which has been so rarely understood — *is* that spiritual meat and drink; and the secret is this: The life which you behold in man, tree or animal is not the Life which is God; human, animal or plant life is not a manifestation of God, and therefore is not immortal, eternal or spiritual. The life of material man or flower is mortal sense objectified: it is a false sense of the Life which is real.

The understanding of this truth will enable you to look away from the objects of sense; it will enable you to refrain from attempting to heal, correct or reform the mortal sense of existence; and as soon as you have conquered the desire to heal or improve the material sense of existence, the spiritual or real begins to unfold and reveal itself to you. You cannot behold or experience eternal Life and its harmonies and beauties while accepting the evidence of the senses as if it were God's creation.

Do not take lightly what I am saying. This is the Great Revelation, Consciousness appearing; Spirit unfolding; Soul revealing itself. The attempt to bring Spirit into operation in this finite sense of existence constitutes the warfare between the flesh and the Spirit. To continue in the belief that by some mental hocus-pocus you are going to make material life perfect; to feel that in some holy way a God or God-power is going to make your human life healthier or lengthier; to dream of some religious magic that will enable you to sail on smoothly in the sea of material living — all this is folly, and it is dangerous. It is leaning on a fable which will not sustain you. The life of material man, the life of the tree, the flower, the animal — this is not the Life eternal; it is not the manifestation of the Life which is God; it is a false, finite, mortal sense of life. Do not attempt to patch up this sense of life; rather turn from it and with your now enlightened consciousness discern the Life which is God; "feel" through your cultivated spiritual sense this divine energy of Spirit; become conscious in the Silence of your Soul powers. *Let* the divine harmonies appear as you disregard the evidence of sight and hearing, tasting, touching and smelling.

Believe me — this is the secret of secrets. This is Life eternal to know this truth. Truly Kings and Emperors would give their thrones could they but learn this one truth, but the rich and powerful in matter — that is, in the material sense of existence — cannot understand this truth; it is to mortal sense too abstract. Just think — there is no value, no reality, no use of struggling for that which is seen and felt — because that is but the unreal concept of eternal values. Can you imagine the power-drunk, the money-mad, the hoarder, the glutton, understanding that what he is handling, saving, fighting and dying for — is shadow — mirage?

That which is real and eternal is not seen or touched, but is spiritually discerned. It is cognized only by the intuitive or inner consciousness. Reality is perceived by the Soul senses, the inner vision.

Only to those who have eyes to see and ears to hear can this vision become a living, vital Presence. Only those who have heard what is said by "the still, small voice" and seen what is visible to the "windows of the Soul" can discern "the temple not made with hands" — the universe of God's creating.

This inner vision, this spiritual consciousness, this Soul sense, comes only in proportion as we accept and realize the great secret: the life of material man, plant or animal is not the eternal Life, God; it is the finite sense — the manifestation of mortal, material sense. This false sense of life must be put off, disregarded, un-valued, in order that the real Life and its formations may become evident and experienced.

Chapter 19
Spiritual Healing

We have seen that for metaphysical healing it is necessary to know:

1. I AM GOD — I exist as infinite spiritual consciousness, embodying within myself the divine idea body, business, home, supply; and my very oneness with God constitutes my oneness with every spiritual idea. Carrying this knowledge into treatment, we realize that regardless of any appearance to the contrary, we are never separate or apart from any form of good.

2. My body is the expression of my spiritual Self or being. It is a reflection of the I that I AM; it is the image and likeness of me and manifests all of the health, harmony, wholeness of the infinite spiritual consciousness which I am. Further, my business, profession, art, or practice likewise is idea, expression or reflection of the qualities and activities of my real perfect being — always spiritually and fruitfully governed and supported.

3. Nature of error. We have learned that the only error or evil is hypnotism, mesmerism, appearing as suggestion or mirage; that when we realize this, the so-called evil — the sin, disease or lack — disappears. We know that error is never person, place, or thing — just mesmerism appearing as person, condition, or circumstance. Mind, or God, being infinite, is the substance and activity of all that appears to us for the moment as error.

4. Very important is the knowledge that the world of sense — that which we see, hear, taste, touch, and smell, that is the structural sense of the universe — it is not the spiritual eternal creation: it is but the finite shadow of God's creation. This wisdom enables us to drop the attempt to heal, correct, change or improve the material sense of life — whether of man, animal or plant; and thus set ourselves free to intuitively "feel" — become conscious of — God's universe. Do not let go of this fourth point until it is a clear reality with you. We cannot take the mortal concept of creation into heaven — harmony. We do not bring God to

the material sense of existence. We surrender the "belief and dream of material living" for the life divine; we exchange the objective sense world for the spiritual formations of divine creation. The physical sense of health includes a heart beating so many times to the minute; a digestive and eliminative system performing at regular intervals; bones, blood, brain — all doing certain things at certain times. Regardless of how perfect these may all be functioning at this moment, this same physical sense says that a continuous disintegration is going on leading to dotage, infirmity and decomposition and death. As opposed to this, the spiritual sense of life shows forth a life and body of eternal substance with no aging, withering, changing conditions — but rather a continuous and successive unfolding of good.

To gain the spiritual awareness of Life and its perfect formations is our purpose in meeting in these pages, We have come together for the one purpose of realizing the God which is Spirit, Soul, Love and eternal life, and to become conscious of the formations and activities of this Life which is God; this Mind which I AM.

Bit by bit we are giving up our concern for the structural universe and in that proportion we are gaining the awareness of the Life which is incorporeal, harmonious and permanent. By devotion to thoughts and things of the Soul, we lose our concern for the thoughts and things of sense. By cultivating our love for God and the world of ideas, we increase our sense of Love and thereby unfold and reveal more of God or good.

As our concern for things of the world lessen, we find ourselves with less anxious thought; and finally instead of thinking thoughts, we become receptive to thoughts and ideas which flow naturally from our Soul to our conscious awareness, We no longer "take thought" to make something happen — but we receive God's thought unfolding good every moment. We no longer give treatments or know the Truth to change some erroneous condition into an harmonious one — but rather, in the face of a discordant note, we become silent and receptive; and the illusion or mirage fades out, and the omnipresent harmony is instantly revealed. This silent receptivity makes way for the conscious realization of the presence and activity of the Messiah.

Omnipotence — omnipresence— is always at hand to guide, direct, lead, govern, support, sustain, maintain, equip. This Universal power is ever-present as our consciousness — but only when the conscious thinking mind is stilled and we are receptive to this omnipresence, do we perceive its activity and fruitage. Omnipresence and omnipotence is not something you have to get, pray for, treat for or desire; it is to be realized through silent receptivity. We need not tell IT what or who is to be benefited. Just be still, be receptive, be patient. The Messiah is the Reality of you and is right where you are — but not discernable through thinking, through either physical or mental force. "Not by might, nor by power, but by my spirit, saith the Lord of hosts." Not by mental power or physical might — but by my Spirit. Do not strive. Do not struggle. "The battle is not yours." Be still. Be quiet. Be patient. Be receptive.

Is there some mist through which you cannot see at the moment; is there a divine harmony hiding behind some ugly or painful mirage; is there a mesmeric sense keeping out the glorious peace of the Soul? Do not contend against it. Do not strike out mentally to do battle with it. The Messiah is here. It is your very own consciousness when human thought is stilled, when human planning and human effort are at an end. Where human effort ends, the activity of the Messiah begins. Where human fear ceases, divine courage begins. Where physical might and mental power end, the divine energy of Spirit begins. When your thought is still, God's thought is revealing, and God's thoughts are quick and powerful.

Make way for the realization of the Presence and Power which is eternally where you are awaiting only your invitation — an invitation which is expressed as Silence, Expectancy, Receptivity.

As the spiritual or intuitive sense becomes more developed, the Messiah is realized as one's higher, or real Self. In proportion as the Messiah becomes more apparent, more consciously with you, It takes over, as it were, and becomes the source, activity and motivating Power and Presence of your experience. Life enters a new phase for you. There are many human ways of achieving success —involving physical and mental prowess. When Spirit animates one, success in any undertaking is the fruit of the Spirit — never the result of human effort. What human steps and actions are called forth are likewise the result of the action of the Spirit.

Spirit is a Presence which is consciously known and felt, and It "feels" as if It were something separate from oneself. Actually, It is the Self — the real Being — but greater than that which appears and walks like a human. This Spirit is that of which the human is a transparency. The Presence always goes before it to prepare the way — to bring about those apparently human circumstances necessary to the achievement.

The conscious awareness of the Spirit is the Messiah which guides and protects every step. It furnishes the wisdom and the supply of all that is needed. The repetition of these words will accomplish nothing. Unless there is an actual awareness, a real contact, a true assurance — there is no performance of spiritual activity.

Awareness of the Presence is a state of Grace. It accomplishes all without labor, anxiety, struggle or strife. Note the ease, simplicity and poise which accompanies the man of Spirit. Watch the effortless energy, the carefree attitude of the one who has achieved contact with the Spirit — with the Soul of himself. Note how the world seems to move in unison with him — all working together for the good of the whole.

Life is a glorious adventure when the Spirit has become a living Reality. Life becomes a thing of now. Concern for the future falls away. Each moment of the day provides its own Grace; its own supply of joy, peace, dominion, home, friendship, success.

Things of "this world" are understood as objects of sense — temporal, finite and temporary — and one does not struggle to get or save these objects.

Do not misunderstand. There is no need for any one to give or throw away savings or investments or insurance. These are a part of today's living and regardless of how great the Spirit is within you, there will be anxious moments for your family if they feel that human wisdom or common sense is breached. But know this: When the Spirit of Truth has been consciously realized, you will never again have concern for the outer welfare; you will know that every moment will fulfill itself with Grace for that moment. You will then see your investments and savings as the "added things" — as evidence of your spiritual development and not as something necessary for a rainy day or old age. Remember, however, that your supply is ever at hand regardless of any material possessions, because your supply is the consciousness of the Presence, and It provides the fullness of good every moment where you are. Do not attempt to hold lightly your savings, insurance or retirement funds, or educational funds for your children — unless you have realized the Master within you. The Master is never a man — but the consciousness of the Spirit of Truth.

Do not belittle human forms of good; and certainly never attempt to take them away from others. As long as an individual needs the physical temple, the book, or any symbol — respect that need. We know that the Sabbath is no more sacred than Tuesday — yet let us keep the Sabbath in quietness and peace out of respect to our neighbor. Even if we do not require hospitals or drugs, let us respect our neighbor's need of them. Even if we have realized the Messiah and no longer need old age pensions and retirement funds, let us respect our neighbor's need of these. Let *your* freedom from the need of these be in your inner realization. Never boast or brag of your freedom from material means — that would be a sure sign you haven't the realization. Let your assurance of permanent Grace be an inner conviction which is outwardly *felt* by those with whom you come in contact. Never voice it except in the closed closet with a student who is on the brink of discovery. It is wiser to *live* your revelation that to speak it.

Live your demonstrated spiritual consciousness and let your living preach it. Do not take your patients or students a step further than they can see at the moment. Always stand by with love, forbearance and forgiveness.

Life becomes an adventure when we realize the presence of the Messiah. No longer is there concern or anxiety for some person "out there" or for some circumstance or condition. Life is now lived one moment at a time and that moment is now and that moment is God's moment.

If your life is not an adventure now; if you are not living in joyous expectancy, a confident assurance, then there is still concern for some one or something "out there" instead of a relaxing in the consciousness that all Life is sustained. You are not necessary to anyone's demonstration of life or security. Your consciousness of this truth would help to set free any whom you may be holding in bondage to the belief of human dependency. When one avenue of supply closes, another opens to fill the moment with God's fullness — as long as one abides by the consciousness of the Presence. The world becomes your playground when you lose fear and concern in the recognition of the presence of the Spirit. Life only begins to be an adventure when we cease living it for ourselves. We are here in this so-called human experience for a reason. We may not clearly discern what that reason is. One thing you may be sure of: Life's purpose is not that we shall live unto ourselves. The adventure only begins when we have found a cause to serve or live for. On lower planes we may live for our family, for the community or nation, or even for a church. We may devote ourselves to education, the care of orphans, or universal peace. All of these are good starting places if the heart, Soul and pocketbook are placed in the work.

Joshua Loth Liebman has said in "Peace of Mind" the following: "There comes a time in the development of ourselves when receiving from others, which is the essence of selfishness, gives way to the irresistible urge to give to others — to grow beyond the limits of one's own skin, whether in the creation of a family or the building of a good society. We reach a point when we become satiated with ourselves and when life demands that we turn outward toward other human life. Then we cease being the passive vessel and ourselves become the living spring. Life does not ask us our wishes in this matter, but in the very process of our own biological maturation it forces us to renounce our status as parasites upon life and summons us to become the patrons of life."

Rising higher there is the ministry of spiritual healing and then teachings the things of the Spirit. At this point you are entering the real activity of Life and are being prepared for more universal opportunity. By this time you have left behind all consideration for your personal self or your own interests and have entered the heart of the Universal and at this point something entirely new enters your experience: the inner world reveals itself to you, and higher forms of service are opened to you.

Chapter 20
Stages of Consciousness

There are not three stages of life — the material, the mental and the spiritual. The material and the mental are one, although they constitute two degrees of the same one. Remember, the material and the mental are one. In this stage thoughts are things; beliefs produce conditions. Ordinarily in metaphysical teaching, the mental and the spiritual are considered one; and therefore, you may have heard or read the term, "mentally spiritual." Be careful of it because it is dangerous to your progress. There is no such thing as *mentally spiritual* because the mental and the physical are two strata or stages of the one; the physical is the more gross; the mental is the higher form, but it is still just a higher form of the material. The proof of this may be seen in such statements as "thoughts are things" and "as a man thinketh so is he," meaning, if he thinks good he will manifest good, and if he thinks evil he will manifest evil. Thinking which produces things and thinking which can produce either good or evil cannot be spiritual.

Notice that nowhere does it say that thinking will produce spirituality. On the contrary, we are told by the greatest spiritual Light, "Which of you by taking thought can add one cubit to his stature?" And from Isaiah, "For my thoughts cannot be your thoughts." In other words, *human* thinking is not spiritual.

Until you realize that the physical and mental realm are one and that one the mortal and material, you will be looking for your good in the wrong place. "Not by might (physical) nor by power (mental) but by my spirit saith the Lord." You are not consciously in the spiritual realm or Kingdom of God, and harmony, until you rise above things and thoughts. If you feel this is difficult you can understand one reason why so few have attained it. Another reason is false teaching. Men have become satisfied when they reached the mental realm, thinking they were in heaven or state of harmony — only to find sooner or later they were leaning on a reed. A day comes when they need a right thought, and it doesn't come, or it doesn't work.

I pray God that you realize you are listening to the deepest wisdom of the ages — the truth about Heaven, harmony. I can reveal this to you and with patience on the part of you and me, I can assist you in its realization — but *you* have to accept, to see, to understand and finally to realize and demonstrate this truth of Truth.

While you are delving around in thoughts — even in good thoughts — you are merely in a higher state of materiality where there are the same opposites: good and evil, health and sickness, life and death, poverty and wealth, discord and harmony. In the spiritual Kingdom there is only infinite, eternal perfection of Life eternal and immortal. In the physical realm, a fall produces a bruise or break; in the mental there is a *belief* of accident producing a *belief* of bruise or break. In the physical, age produces loss of faculties, of teeth, of vitality; in the mental the *belief* of age produces these same physical discords.

In spiritual consciousness none of these mental beliefs are found nor any of their physical out picturing. The spiritual realm has neither beliefs nor conditions — just the eternal grace of divine Being.

Probably when you first studied Truth, you found it a difficult thing to rise above the physical to the mental; no doubt you struggled with yourself to learn that physical effects had mental causes. Now you have achieved it —and I tell you that you have merely attained a higher state of materiality. I tell you that the physical and the mental are two stages of one and that one mortal and material. Now you must rise above things and thoughts.

What difference does it make whether it is because of a *belief* that green apples cause cramps — or just because of green apples themselves. You still have cramps to eliminate from thought and green apples to eliminate from the body. At this point you will ask what to do or think in case the green apples produce cramps. The moment you have the realm of things and thoughts, they will have no effect — or probably you won't eat them. For the moment, realize that neither the apples nor the belief about them is power, because of the First Commandment, "Thou shalt have no other gods before me," and you know this Me is Spirit; therefore, the *only* Power is the *one* Power and I AM that one. What power has either the apple or the belief since I AM the law — the only law unto both apples and beliefs? Do you remember that you were given dominion over the things of the earth and the thoughts of the above, or mental realm? You are the law, and neither things nor thoughts can govern, control or affect you.

Remember that stating this Truth is not power — is not the healer; this Truth itself, unstated, is the Power and Presence. This Truth would be the only factor in your existence now but for the acceptance of duality — a selfhood apart from God.

What is the spiritual Kingdom or consciousness like, since you have never tasted or touched it in the realm of things or thoughts? That is our next step of realization and you will attain it in proportion to your ability to release yourself from "taking thought."

One thing is certain: spiritual consciousness is not going to patch up your outworn human experience; it is not going to doctor your ills or add dollars to your income (though it may appear to do just those very things): No — spiritual consciousness will manifest itself in a completely new, vital, spiritual, eternal existence and only the world of humans will see it as improved human hood. You will see it as it really is — omnipresence.

BN Publishing

Improving People's Life

www.bnpublishing.com

Breinigsville, PA USA
09 December 2009
228923BV00003B/28/P